Contents

Museum and Historic Site Management

About the Series

The American Association for State and Local History Book Series publishes technical and professional information for those who practice and support history, and addresses issues critical to the field of state and local history. To submit a proposal or manuscript to the series, please request proposal guidelines from AASLH headquarters: AASLH Editorial Board, 1717 Church St., Nashville, Tennessee 37203. Telephone: (615) 320-3203. Website: www.aaslh.org.

About the Organization

The American Association for State and Local History (AASLH) is a national history organization headquartered in Nashville, Tennessee. AASLH provides leadership and support for its members who preserve and interpret state and local history in order to make the past more meaningful to all Americans. AASLH is a membership association representing history organizations and the professionals who work in them. AASLH members are leaders in preserving, researching, and interpreting traces of the American past to connect the people, thoughts, and events of yesterday with the creative memories and abiding concerns of people, communities, and our nation today. In addition to sponsorship of this book series, AASLH publishes *History News* magazine, a newsletter, technical leaflets and reports, and other materials; confers prizes and awards in recognition of outstanding achievement in the field; and supports a broad education program and other activities designed to help members work more effectively. To join AASLH, go to www.aaslh.org or contact Membership Services, AASLH, 1717 Church St., Nashville, TN 37203.

Museum and Historic Site Management

A Case Study Approach

Samantha Chmelik

ROWMAN & LITTLEFIELD
Lanham • Boulder • New York • London

Published by Rowman & Littlefield
A wholly owned subsidiary of The Rowman & Littlefield Publishing Group, Inc.
4501 Forbes Boulevard, Suite 200, Lanham, Maryland 20706
www.rowman.com

Unit A, Whitacre Mews, 26-34 Stannary Street, London SE11 4AB, United Kingdom

British Library Cataloguing in Publication Information Available

Library of Congress Cataloging-in-Publication Data Is Available

ISBN 978-1-4422-5637-8 (cloth: alk. paper)
ISBN 978-1-4422-5638-5 (paperback: alk. paper)
ISBN 978-1-4422-5639-2 (electronic)

♾™ The paper used in this publication meets the minimum requirements of American
National Standard for Information Sciences—Permanence of Paper for Printed Library
Materials, ANSI/NISO Z39.48-1992.

Printed in the United States of America

List of Tables

Acknowledgments

The people who directly and indirectly contributed to this book are too numerous to individually list. The perspectives and experiences of my museum colleagues from the Richard H. Driehaus Museum and the International Museum of Surgical Science, volunteer colleagues at Czech history societies and the National Civic Art Society, and fellow graduate school students at the University of Illinois at Chicago and Loyola University, Chicago, informed the cases and their protagonists. The enthusiasm and encouragement of my editor Charles Harmon spurred me to develop rich, complex cases and question sets.

On a personal note, some of my earliest memories are of my parents taking my brother and me to visit museums. My mother preferred the art and history museums, while my father liked the science and natural history museums. We all enjoyed the planetariums and zoos. As I see my brother and sister-in-law take my nephews to museums, I hope those visits spark the lifelong curiosity that opened new worlds and possibilities to my brother and me. I dedicate this book to all of the children and families who are inspired by the creativity and passion of museum professionals.

Introduction

The roots of this book were formed in the early 1980s when I visited the Lincoln-Tallman House during a school field trip. Subsequently, I visited as many museums, historic homes, and historic sites as I could—even keeping a log of my visits. The stories of the objects and occupants and the behind-the-scenes management of sites fascinated me. After volunteering at different types of nonprofit organizations, running a research business, and working at museums, the satisfaction and challenges of working at such institutions were immediately apparent. During my MBA studies, the use of case studies introduced students to scenarios and issues across different functions and industries. We had the opportunity to see a problem and its solutions from multiple perspectives and across different timeframes. As I studied for a master's degree in public history, I thought the case study approach would be applicable, too.

Case studies help hone analytical and decision-making skills. You see multiple people interpret a problem and offer differing solutions. In a classroom setting, you may be asked to argue a point of view that is different from your own. Understanding that different point of view teaches you to consider a situation through various lenses and understand why someone else may have a different perspective or solution. Then you can address those points in your own arguments.

For those in the field, case studies can help you anticipate similar situations at your own institution and develop your own response before the situation arises. All of these cases studies are based on situations that occurred at actual museums, historic sites, and other nonprofit organizations. A case study may include multiple events that happened at different institutions to force the protagonists into action. Those complications also force you to develop a more thorough response—there are no quick fixes or band-aids. Solutions are also not provided. The goal of each case is not to find the one correct solution, but to understand the challenges inherent in developing a solution. In the real world, your decision today may change tomorrow, due to an unforeseen event.

Your role within an institution will also change over time. If you become a director, you will have to make decisions about issues and departments that are not your area of expertise. Defining a problem correctly and then investigating possible solutions are universal skills.

BOOK METHODOLOGY

The case studies are fictionalized representations of real-life situations that have occurred at museums, historic sites, and nonprofit organizations. Some situations are drawn from personal experience; others were uncovered via research. Elements from multiple situations are incorporated into each individual case study to create multifaceted scenarios which challenge you to develop a creative yet pragmatic solution.

The case studies read like a story, embedding you in the fictionalized museum or historic site. This book contains ten chapters and each chapter has three case studies. A chapter begins with an introduction that contextualizes the topic at hand and ends with an epilogue that summarizes the core problems at the heart of the cases.

The individual cases begin with a synopsis of the issue which includes an introduction to the protagonists. Next, a background of the institution provides relevant data like

- institutional history;
- financial data;
- attendance statistics;
- location demographics;
- collection overview; and
- protagonist introductions.

Then the situation unfolds and the protagonists begin their dialogues. The case ends with one or more of the protagonists tasked with recommending a solution to the problem. They are required to answer three to four questions in their recommendation. An additional set of three questions is provided to probe other issues. The protagonists are bound by their points of view, experiences, and education. They may misinterpret a problem or lack a resource that you may have. When considering your responses to the questions, think about the options for the protagonists and for yourself.

Art museums, historical societies, science museums, historic homes, botanic gardens, planetariums, history museums, and children's museums are all settings for the cases. Institutions of various sizes, ages, and budgets are represented. The protagonists are museum and public history professionals and volunteers at various stages of their careers. The chapters have three main clusters:

1. General Management: Board Management, Fundraising, Personnel Management;
2. Key Departments and Functions: Collection Management, Exhibition Planning, Programs and Education, Community Engagement; and
3. Key Tools: Marketing, Technology, Financial Planning.

This book begins with the overarching management issues, moves into specific departments, and ends with cross-functional impacts. The chapters can be read in any order or separately. You may also choose to read the cases that are set in an institution similar to your own, that is, an art museum or a historical society. Since communication and human nature are the cores of the dilemmas in all of the case studies, the case issues can be translated into institutions of any type or size.

THE CASE STUDY APPROACH

Case studies are designed to help you develop the following skills:

- defining a problem;
- identifying potential solutions;
- understanding the pros and cons of each solution;
- selecting the most effective solution to the problem; and
- persuading others to support your solution.

The final step of persuasion is critical. A case study or real-life problem might have several viable solutions. You have to persuade your audience that your solution is the most effective for the current circumstances. For that reason, the "correct" solutions to the cases in this book are not provided. Devising the solution may seem like the natural stopping point, and we may think that others will come to the same conclusions as we do. Each of these cases ends with the protagonists preparing to persuade others to share their point of view. Before the persuasion begins the protagonists must answer a series of questions. At that stage, you conduct research to support or form your point of view.

RESOURCES

Museum, historic site, and nonprofit professionals may already be familiar with the associations and publications listed in the bibliography or referred to in the cases. If you belong to a professional association, like the American Alliance of Museums (AAM), American Association for State and Local History (AASLH), National Council on Public History, a regional museum association, or discipline-specific association, then you will already have access to ethics guidelines, best practices and standards, LinkedIn groups, association forums, technical bulletins, and other materials which will help you define issues, identify potential solutions, and ask other professionals' opinions.

Depending on the problem, consulting materials from other professional associations (e.g., the Association for Professional Fundraisers), or research organizations (e.g., the Pew Research Center), might also be helpful. Your local public librarian or the librarian for a professional association can point you toward the appropriate resources. After completing your research, developing your point of view, and formulating your solution, you must persuade others to support your solution.

Some problems may require the assistance of experts, such as lawyers, accountants, architects, or preservationists. Issues of ownership, personnel management, and policy/procedure development usually have a legal component. An accountant can answer questions about tax implications, proper money handling procedures, and financial planning. Some institutions may recruit such professionals for their boards or have them on retainer. Professional associations like the American Bar Association or American Institute of Certified Public Accountants (AICPA) can help you identify lawyers, accountant lawyers, and accountants who specialize in nonprofit organizations.

DECISION MAKING AND PERSUASION

Research may uncover additional problems and issues for consideration. Focusing on the actual problem is critical. First, you must define that problem and then decide your solution(s). Three books in the bibliography will help you hone your problem-solving, decision-making, and communication skills: *Execution*, *Selling the Invisible*, and *Warfighting*.

Execution: The Discipline of Getting Things Done by Larry Bossidy and Ram Charan is a classic management book. Bossidy and Charan provide structures and tactics for managing people, constructing a strategic review, and implementing objectives. Their lessons can be applied to any type of organization.

Bossidy and Charan posit that good leaders are interested in all aspects of their organizations and engage in dialogue with all staff. When difficult conversations need to occur, personal connections have already been established, so participants then feel that they are engaged in a conversation, not an interrogation. Good leaders are also realistic about available resources, personal competencies, and the skills and talents of their colleagues and themselves. That realistic assessment should inform clear goals and priorities that are communicated with the entire staff. As you will see in most of the case studies, the lack of personal connections among staff and/or the board, unrealistic assumptions, and unclear goals or strategies cause the problems.

Harry Beckwith's *Selling the Invisible* is subtitled *A Field Guide to Modern Marketing*. While marketers will learn a number of techniques to help them with their jobs, Beckwith is teaching everyone communication skills. His teachings about clarity of language, properly defining a problem, and listening to others are cross-applicable.

Like Bossidy and Charan, Beckwith recognizes that the relationships among people, based on an understanding of individual needs, determine the success or failure of an organization. Beckwith extends that relationship to customers/visitors/guests. He believes that if you understand people and general human behavior, you can improve your communication skills and persuade people to use your service. Some of the institutions in the case studies are disconnected from their communities and consequently seeing a decline in attendance or donations.

The US Marine Corp's *Warfighting* may seem like an odd choice, but it is the most concise, pragmatic decision-making tutorial available. The book also recognizes that the leader cannot be everywhere, so everyone should be trained in decision-making skills. Success for any initiative depends on preparation, organization, flexibility, and an understanding of human nature.

Its distinction between preparing for war and conducting war reminds us that creating a plan or crafting a solution is different than the actual execution of the plan/solution. We have to be prepared for the problems that could occur when enacting our plans/solutions. This book reminds us that situations are fluid and uncertain. As you are working on the situation to one problem, circumstances change, and you are facing a new problem or new issues from the original problem. That's why these case studies do not provide specific solutions. The point is to learn how to make decisions based on the situation at hand.

ANALYTICAL TOOLS

Analytical tools help you clarify your thoughts and consider your options. The classic pros and cons list helps you define your problem and identify and rank potential solutions. The business world offers other analytical tools that can aid the decision-making process. Using these analytical tools may also prove persuasive to board members and non-museum professionals, who probably use them in their own businesses. The Blindspot Analysis, SWOT (Strength-Weakness-Opportunity-Threat) Analysis, and Risk Mitigation Plan facilitate the analysis of data and situations, as well as considering the repercussions of actions.

Blindspot Analysis was originally conceived by Michael Porter and developed by Benjamin Gilad. Blindspot Analysis attempts to identify and ameliorate flaws, assumptions, and inaccuracies that adversely affect strategies and decisions. Table I.1 lists the seven sources of blindspots and their definitions.

Blindspots may prevent an organization from recognizing a problem or enacting a solution. Identifying and communicating the blindspots acknowledges their existence and their power. People may still choose to support their blindspot, but they do so understanding the risk.

The SWOT analysis is widely used and misused. Its purpose is to assess the current situation of an organization, a department, a specific program, and/or a strategy. First, you define the issue to be analyzed, for example, the museum should move from paid to suggested admission. Listing the different issues under each component is the first step in the SWOT analysis. Once you have completed the boxes in Table I.2, then you analyze their impact on one another and rank those impacts.

You may find it helpful to complete multiple SWOTs for the same issue, but from different perspectives. Building a new wing poses different challenges for the board, the institution's director, the fundraising department, and the marketing department, among others.

Table I.1   Blindspot Analysis

Invalid Assumptions	Winner's Curse	Escalating Commitment	Constrained Perspective	Over-confidence	Information Filtering	Educated Incapacity
Organizational Myths or Unchecked Facts	Overpayment to Achieve Objectives	Pride/Fear Prevents Loss-Cutting	Overestimate Risk	Overestimate Expertise and Knowledge	Misinterpretation of Information	Experience-Created Bias

Table I.2   SWOT Analysis

Strengths	Weaknesses
1. Strength One:	1. Weakness One:
2. Strength Two:	2. Weakness Two:
3. Strength Three:	3. Weakness Three:
Opportunities	*Threats*
1. Opportunity One:	1. Threat One:
2. Opportunity Two:	2. Threat Two:
3. Opportunity Three:	3. Threat Three:

Table I.3   Risk Mitigation Plan

Risk	Severity	Probability	Warning Signs	Plan
Summarize the risk	Low/Medium/High	Low/Medium/High	Identify the signals that will warn you when the risk is occurring	Create potential solutions to mitigate the risk

After using the SWOT and Blindspot Analysis to define your problem and consider solutions, you should have created your list of solutions. Then you can use a Risk Mitigation Plan to anticipate risks, assess probabilities, and create action plans to mitigate the risks, as shown in Table I.3.

Identifying every possible risk and accurately assessing the severity or probability is challenging. Focus on the most probable risks and their effect on mission, institutional reputation, personnel, and budget. Working through these tables as a group exercise could be counterproductive. If each person completes their tables and shares their perspectives at a group meeting, personal blindspots should be obviated, and the strongest, most realistic assessments should emerge. Then a presentation can be created.

THE NON-DECISION DECISION

After considering the options and using the analytical tools, it is possible to decide to do nothing at the present time. A premature decision can be as harmful as a bad decision. If you believe that the protagonists do not have enough information to make a solid decision or that the situation is still evolving, the solution may be to wait for additional information or reactions. Interim or incremental decisions may also be used to address an immediate, temporary need, while simultaneously providing the protagonist with the flexibility to consult experts, conduct additional research, or wait for emotions to subside. The best decisions are thoughtful, not hasty. A good case study employs facts, best practices, ethics, and emotional responses to ground readers in the complexity of the workplace and to induce self-reflection.

A TEACHING NOTE

The chapters and case studies follow a consistent format, so they can be used singularly in a classroom setting or as a professional development activity at an institution. The cases are most appropriate for graduate students in museum studies, public history, or nonprofit management classes. Undergraduates may also benefit from using the cases to learn about the issues involved in managing museums or historic site. Institutional directors or human resources departments could also use the cases to train new professionals or to stimulate internal discussions about professional issues.

As previously discussed, the chapter introductions define the topic (i.e., board management), offer any needed definitions, and contextualize the topic. Each case begins with a synopsis and then moves into the institutional background, protagonist introduction, issue presentation, and dialogues. The cases conclude with two sets of three to four questions. The first question set directly relates to the issue at hand and the second question set might also be considered when forming a response.

The principle objective for the class to understand is the complexity of decision-making in real-life situations. A second objective for the class to evaluate is their personal skill levels at defining problems, identifying solutions, selecting solutions, and persuading others to enact their solution. These cases can also be used to help students identify their risk tolerance, communication styles, and career objectives by immersing them in the daily lives of museum and historic site professionals.

CASE SELECTION

Complementary and supplementary are two different strategies that can be used to select a case or cases for classroom use. A complementary strategy uses cases in the same subject area as the class to coordinate with the other readings and class projects. An exhibition design class may benefit from selecting exhibition planning cases or marketing/financial planning cases that focus on exhibitions.

A supplementary strategy uses cases from a different subject area to broaden the student's perspective. Assigning a board management case study to an exhibition design class illustrates how board decisions are made and impact individual departments.

The broader curricula of museum management or introduction to public history classes provide the opportunity to use multiple cases from different chapters and can be used to complement or supplement existing readings and class projects. If students have had difficulties with certain topics, the immersive nature of the case study may prove illuminating. Reading about best practices in board management is necessary; a case study shows how to apply that knowledge.

TEACHING THE CASE

Using the group presentation technique to teach the case underscores the messages of teamwork and persuasion that pervade the cases. Though the following instructions may need to be adjusted based on class size, class length, and other assignments in the syllabus, the general instructions should be observed.

The class should be divided into groups of four. Two groups are assigned the same case, for example Group A and Group B must prepare chapter 4, case 2. Each group reads their case and prepares their answers to the questions at the end of the case, culminating in their solution for resolving the issue presented. For the class discussion, each group crafts a presentation using PowerPoint, Prezi, or another tool. Other handouts or mockups may also be created, per the group's discretion.

Each group will present their solution and then be questioned by the other group. Presenting the solution in the slide/visual format might be challenging for students. The Why-Why-Why technique should help them concisely summarize and present their solution. Why-Why-Why presents the answer and then three layers of rationales, for example:

The board should reduce the equipment budget by 20 percent.

- Why? The budget overestimated the equipment costs.
- Why? The department coordinator obtained only one quote.
- Why? There is no policy about how many quotes should be obtained.

The museum director and department heads should institute a policy that requires at least two competitive bids for equipment purchases.

- Why? The department head almost overpaid for new equipment.
- Why? No bid policy exists.
- Why? No one realized that the institution could be overpaying for equipment.

The oral presentations will provide additional details and reasons for each one of the answers and the logic that links the answers.

Since each case typically has three to five main protagonists, individuals in the questioner group may wish to take on the personas of the protagonists when questioning the presenters. After each group has presented and questioned one another, the class questions both groups and then votes on their preferred solution. A broader class discussion may ensue afterward.

Table I.4   Class Presentation Time Table

Time Table	Activity
15 to 20 minutes	Group A presents
5 to 10 minutes	Group B questions Group A
15 to 20 minutes	Group B presents
5 to 10 minutes	Group A questions Group B
15 to 20 minutes	The class questions both groups
5 minutes	The class votes on which group has the better solution
20 to 30 minutes	The class discusses other potential solutions

Assuming a two and a half hour class and leaving time for other issues, a general schedule would be as presented in Table I.4.

This format shows the students how many different solutions can be proposed to one problem and how important communication skills are.

CASE EVALUATION AND GRADING

The presentation document itself, oral arguments, and questions from each group member should be evaluated. The document must address the first three questions at the end of the case and should acknowledge or address the second set of three questions. The arguments should present their thesis and supporting points, using the Why-Why-Why response technique.

The oral arguments and questions can be evaluated on basic presentation skills, that is, voice projection and eye contact, relevance to the case under discussion, and the logic or coherence of the question or response.

A group assessment and a self-assessment will also help students learn to articulate their strengths and areas for improvement, which they will need to do in personnel evaluations at their future jobs.

The weight of each grading element is at the discretion of the individual professor. Requiring the use of other course materials is also an option.

ALTERNATIVE CASE TEACHING METHOD: PAPER

Time constraints may preclude class presentations. Case analyses can also be assigned as papers. The students could pick a case or be assigned a case. They would research the issue and write their solution in the classic term paper style:

- Introduction: address the topic, state the thesis, define the paper scope;
- Body: prove the thesis with researched examples and logical arguments; and
- Conclusion: restate the thesis and summarize the main arguments.

Students should address the arguments raised by the different protagonists and explain why their solution is preferable. A paper provides the opportunity for a student to incorporate additional research, including interviews with museum and historic site professionals and other class materials. The length of the paper can be adjusted according to the other class assignments and the incorporation of other materials. A classic term paper should be at least ten pages, excluding the bibliography.

ALTERNATIVE CASE TEACHING METHOD: CLASS DISCUSSION

If presentations and long papers are incompatible with the other assignments, class discussion is another option. Everyone in the class would be assigned to read the same case or an entire chapter, selected per the *Case Selection* suggestions, and to develop their answers to the first three questions or all of the questions, per the instructor's discretion and time constraints. A ten-minute introduction to the case by the instructor should explain the reason for selecting the case, describe the link between the case and the other class readings and assignments, review the major issues of the case, and ask one of the case questions to spark discussion. Either the instructor or a student may act as a facilitator to move along the discussion during the conversational lulls. If multiple cases have been assigned, the students could be asked to apply the questions raised in case 1 to case 2 or to compare and contrast the responses of different protagonists to the individual cases, that is, how would Protagonist A from case 1 respond to the issues in case 2.

Alternatively, after the introduction, the class could be broken into teams of three to five students to discuss their individual responses to the case and then develop a team response for presentation to the class. After the group presentations, the class can discuss the solutions presented. During the conclusion, the instructor can review the key learnings that emerged during the class period and tie those learnings to other assignments. A suggested schedule for a class discussion with team breakout, assuming a two and a half hour long class, would be as presented in Table I.5.

Table I.5   Class Discussion Time Table

Time Table	Activity
10 minutes	Introduction
30 minutes	Individual Group Discussions
5 minutes per group	Group Presentations, approximately three to five groups
20 minutes	Class Discussion
10 minutes	Conclusion

The times can be adjusted to accommodate additional case discussion or a shorter class period. Allowing time for both small group and class discussion will help students experience the same constructs as the cases themselves: discussions with a small group of staff or board members that then lead to an eventual presentation to a larger group.

READING THE BOOK

Regardless of the teaching method used, students and professionals will benefit from the immersive nature of the cases which challenge their points of view and require potentially difficult action plans. All of the cases provide an avenue to think about how individuals and institutions react to challenges and uncertainties. The success of any institution depends on individuals working together for a common purpose and agreeing on a set of governing principles. As you will read, conflict and problems result when people disagree about the institution's purpose or its operational methodology. For those situations sparked by external factors, internal unity may be tested but is needed to implement the institutional response. Consider those internal and external pressures as you read each case and develop your solutions.

Chapter 1

Board Management

INTRODUCTION

The dynamic between the board and the museum director determines the institution's success at fulfilling its mission. While the two parties must agree on the mission, they should have constructive disagreements about fulfilling that mission. A board and a museum director who always agree about strategy and tactics can be a sign of a stagnant institution. A board and a museum director who always disagree create a dysfunctional institution. Constructive communication, brainstorming, and defined expectations demonstrate the happy medium that enables a successful dynamic.

This chapter features three case studies exploring:

- board recruitment;
- museum director management;
- staff-board interactions;
- community relations; and
- board giving obligations.

The interpersonal relationships between the staff and the board impact how the issues are contextualized and defined. While the boundaries between board and staff responsibilities may vary according to the particulars of your institution, those boundaries must be clear to both the board and the staff. As you develop solutions to the questions asked at the end of each case study, consider how those relationships affect the viability of the solutions.

1

CASE 1: GERDES CHILDREN'S MUSEUM

Every May, Jane Harwick, the chair of the board, and Carlene Nicholas, the director of the Gerdes Children's Museum, review each board member's progress toward meeting his or her giving obligation. At the June board meeting, each board member receives a thank-you note with a graphic recognizing their contribution to that point and reminding them of any outstanding contributions needed before the end of the fiscal year on September 30. The board does not have an official warning policy for members who have fallen behind in their giving prior to the deadline. When a popular board member appears to be in danger of losing his board seat, Nicholas and Harwick think about creating a formal warning policy.

Gerdes Children's Museum Background

Charles Gerdes was an engineer at a US government federally funded research and development facility during the 1950s and 1960s. The Gerdes were a founding family of Adamsville and had amassed a small fortune from real estate investments. Charles and his contemporaries were the generation who inherited the last of the Gerdes fortune. Civic-minded Charles had searched for a way to use his inheritance to help the town. Inspired by Sputnik, Charles resolved that the children of Adamsville would always have the opportunity to learn about math and science. He used his inheritance to establish the Gerdes Children's Museum and its endowment.

The museum was instantly popular with the community. Members of other prominent families clamored to join the board. Like the Gerdes, their social prominence typically outweighed their financial contributions. Over time, the board's investments in construction projects and traveling exhibits had depleted the endowment. Consequently, fundraising and board giving became a serious concern.

Giving Obligation Policy

Ten years ago, the Gerdes Children's Museum had minimal cash reserves, no development strategy, and a disengaged board. The Gerdes was well attended and well regarded in the community. Its financial woes were also well-known. Revenue from attendance and the museum store covered 40 percent of the operating budget. The Gerdes family contributed another 20 percent. Random contributions and ad hoc fundraising campaigns sometimes met the shortfall.

Prior to Carlene's arrival, the board consisted of community leaders, members of prominent local families, and teachers. A board seat at the Gerdes was considered either a crowning achievement after a long career or a community service obligation.

Fearing the museum's closure after multiple years of budget shortfalls, the community pressured the board to create a long-term financial strategy for the Gerdes. The search for a museum director with extensive fundraising experience ensued. Carlene impressed the board with her plans for annual giving programs, grants, and board giving obligations. Carlene recognized that the teachers had limited financial resources and proposed board giving requirements that incorporated cash donations, volunteer hours, in-kind donations, and membership recruitment. Carlene was hired by the board because of her fundraising success. Instituting a board giving requirement was a condition of her acceptance.

Though a few board members resigned after Carlene's hiring, her plan proved successful. As board members contributed time and money, the community also participated in annual fund drives. The museum received a few grants and was able to hire two part-time educators. The new cash reserve fund contained one year's worth of operating expenses. The Gerdes was on firm financial footing for the first time in decades.

When Jane and Carlene met annually to review the board contributions before the June meeting, the individual board members had typically reached 70–80 percent of their annual contribution. They appreciated the thank you reminders at the beginning of the fourth quarter and looked forward to the creative graphics that Carlene used to acknowledge their contributions.

Current Year Review

"The train cars were a big hit last year," said Jane. "I thought the guys were going to start playing choo-choo."

Carlene laughed and said, "Kathy did a great job creating those graphics. Much more fun than giving everyone a thermometer or balance sheet."

"We've done trains, blocks, and food. What else?"

"Next year is the antique doll exhibit. We could do dresses for girl dolls and suits for boy dolls."

"I love it," said Jane. "We probably should do the evaluations now. See how many dresses and suits everyone has contributed."

"Overall, looks like we are on track," said Carlene.

"Ha, ha," said Jane.

The first six reviews had gone well. The board members were at 80 percent of their obligation. Four reviews remained. Tom Klaus was next. As a member of a prominent family who also had ties to the namesake Gerdes family, Tom's support of Carlene had been critical after her arrival. Tom usually contributed 80–90 percent of his annual amount by May.

Carlene began reviewing Tom's file.

"That frown concerns me," said Jane.

Carlene picked up the phone and called Toni, the museum's administrative assistant. "Do we have all the volunteer log sheets? Can you double check? Can you re-run the board giving reports? . . . Oh, ok. Thanks."

Carlene sighed and said, "Tom has only given $1,000 since last September. Toni pulled all the reports this morning."

"Are you sure?" asked Jane. "Didn't he volunteer at the holiday party? I thought he donated the magnifying glasses for the forensics program."

"No, that was Tom Burke. Tom K. had the flu and couldn't come to the holiday party."

The women sat quietly for a few minutes.

Jane said, "I haven't heard anything about financial difficulties or health problems. He was excited about the annual tadpole counting program."

"Yeah," said Carlene. "I saw him a couple of weeks ago. He didn't try to avoid me like Rupert did."

Rupert was a board member who wanted to leave the board but felt familial pressure to remain. Once Carlene understood the situation, she asked Rupert if he wanted to be the honorary chair of the annual holiday party—a solution that satisfied everyone.

"If Tom doesn't meet his obligation by September 30, he is automatically off the board," said Jane. "What's our warning policy?"

"Well," Carlene said, "we didn't include a warning policy in the board member agreement. They know the September 30 deadline. We started the progress reports because people asked for an update before summer started."

"I don't want to embarrass him at the full board meeting," said Jane. "He's a great ambassador for the Gerdes. He usually gives cash or an in-kind. If he's having financial problems, maybe we should remind him about the volunteering option."

Carlene said, "We have to be fair. We've set the precedent of the annual progress reports presented in front of everyone at the board meeting. We both like Tom, but we can't let that create favoritism. Everyone agreed that peer pressure keeps the board from slipping back to its old ways."

"I know we have to be fair. Maybe Tom just lost track of his contributions or will bring a check to the meeting. He still has until the end of September."

"Plenty of time left," agreed Carlene.

As the women completed the remaining progress reports, they agreed that the board giving requirement policy needed more procedures and decided to recommend a codified board giving progress report system. The recommendations to the board must answer the following questions:

1. Why is a formal board giving progress report system needed?
2. Should giving milestones be required throughout the year, rather than at the end of the year? Why? Why not?

3. If multiple milestones are established, what are the consequences of failing to meet those milestones?
4. How often will progress reports be distributed? Should progress reports be presented privately or publicly?

Other questions to consider:

1. Are Jane and Carlene overreacting to Tom's atypical giving? Are they solving an actual problem?
2. What are the potential consequences if the board decides not to institute a formal progress report system?
3. Should board members receive warning notices if their giving is below a certain percentage at specific times over the course of the fiscal year?

CASE 2: BURMILANA COUNTY HISTORICAL SOCIETY

The Burmilana County Historical Society board hired its first full-time museum director, Gail Burr, in June. Gail had graduated with a master's degree in public history that June. She had volunteered at the historical society since she was a teenager and was well liked in the community. After years of dwindling government support, the board was transitioning from a community board to a donor board to ensure the financial stability of the historical society. The board had been thrilled to hire Gail, but recognized her management inexperience and assigned a board member as her mentor. Some of the historical society volunteers have expressed concerns about Gail's recent decisions to board members. As the first quarterly board meeting approaches, the board prepares to discuss the volunteer discontent with Gail.

Burmilana County Historical Society History

Established in 1879, the Burmilana County Historical Society preserved and memorialized the people and traditions of the small towns scattered throughout Burmilana County. The Burmilana County Historical Society was located in the town of Burmilana, population 5,700. Located on Main Street, the three-story building presented exhibits on the first and second floors. The research library was also on the second floor. Community meeting rooms were in the basement, and the staff office and workspaces were on the third floor. The collection contained photographs, political campaign memorabilia, old signs, tools, assorted household items, and clothes. Schoolchildren were obliged to visit during fourth and eleventh grades. Excluding the school visitors, regular visitation averaged three hundred people per year. The board developed the exhibit plans and tour scripts, based on feedback from the volunteers who then conducted the tours and executed the exhibits.

The volunteers generally fell into two categories: retired residents who loved history and teenagers who loved history and/or needed an extracurricular activity for their college application. Other town residents helped during the semi-annual cleaning or provided in-kind services. The regular volunteer corps numbered between ten and fifteen people, with one-third being teenagers.

Esprit de corps (a feeling of pride) was a board priority. Volunteers signed an agreement, committing to a specified number of hours and to the Burmilana County Historical Society Code of Conduct. The rare volunteer who violated the agreement was immediately asked to leave. Only five volunteers had been asked to leave since the code's adoption sixty years ago.

Prior to Gail, the board had managed the historical society with a different member acting as on-site manager every day. The majority of the funding came from Burmilana County. After multiple years of a declining economy, the county reduced its contribution of the budget from 90 percent to 10 percent. The board decided that fundraising should become its main objective and began the search for a full-time director.

The board and the town hoped for someone like Gail as the first director, a local resident educated in museum management. Gail began volunteering at the historical society when she was a high school sophomore. Willing to conduct five consecutive school tours and to kill large bugs, Gail was respected by her fellow volunteers. Gail also belonged to the subgroup of volunteers who believed in "doing things the right way" and would spend hours researching "the right way." Other volunteers valued the quick completion of project using their traditional means over best practices. The board member on duty arbitrated the issue of the moment, underscoring the value placed on compromise.

When Gail returned home during college and grad school vacations, she always volunteered at the historical society. As her June graduation date approached, several volunteers asked the board to hire Gail as the director. Her work ethic and dedication impressed everyone. She had successfully managed exhibit installations and the teenage volunteers. She had created budgets and even generated donations. Thus, the board agreed that Gail was an excellent choice for director and offered her the position.

Gail's Vision

Museum director of the Burmilana County Historical Society was Gail's dream job. She was thrilled and overwhelmed when offered the position. Her mind overflowed with all the programs, exhibitions, and changes that she wanted to implement. She believed that the Burmilana County Historical Society hadn't fully realized the potential of its collection. The photographs alone told rich stories, including the creation of Works Progress Administration (WPA) murals. If she wrote a grant, the photos could be digitized and used by scholars all over the world.

"Don't be too gangbusters," warned Gail's mom. "Some of the volunteers have worked there since before you were born. They love it as much as you do. Don't throw everything away in the first week. You need to teach people how you want something done and why. The volunteers are there to help you, and you need to help them."

Gail listened to her mother's concerns and was sure that everyone would understand her plans. First, she had to update the exhibits, or even mothball some exhibits. The misspellings on labels had never been corrected.

"Part of the charm," said some volunteers.

"Amateur," thought Gail. "You know it's wrong. Fix it."

After Gail accepted the position, the board asked her to create a list of major projects and initiatives with recommendations and an action plan. At the first quarterly meeting, Gail and the board would then review Gail's report, the budget, future financial needs, and then prioritize the projects. Gail had written her report. She considered updating labels a small project and a personal priority. As a volunteer, Gail had not been allowed to correct or update the labels. As director, label updates were her priority.

Since Gail lacked management experience, she and the board agreed that a board mentor would be extremely helpful. Bryan, the owner of the local hardware store, was selected. Closer in age to Gail than the other board members, Bryan was a lifelong Burmilana County resident and understood the difficulties that Gail might have being perceived as an adult by people who knew her when she was a baby. Some of Bryan's part-time teenage employees also volunteered at the historical society. Gail welcomed Bryan's mentorship and acknowledged that being the manager of people who had babysat her was a bit strange. The two met for lunch every other week to work on the board report and discuss any problems.

Volunteer Discontent

"All of our labels are gone," wailed Mrs. Stafford. "She threw them all away and kept talking about Serrell standards. I don't know what she means."

Mrs. Stafford's statement of distress was Bryan's first clear indication that Gail needed more mentoring. Initially, Gail and the older volunteers worked well together. Some were secretly optimistic that the labels would finally be corrected. Other people commented that Gail was a bit impatient when asked why a particular technique should be used. Bryan and Gail discussed using the seven second rule before replying to questions. Gail initially waited three seconds but had recently progressed to five seconds.

"She was getting ready to trash all the holiday decorations, until Mrs. Blake asked to have them. Mrs. Green freaked because now the window won't be right," offered TJ, one of Bryan's teenage employees and a museum volunteer. For each holiday, the buildings on Main Street, including the historical society, coordinated their holiday decorations.

Bryan was surprised that Gail would disregard such a cherished tradition. He took her out to lunch to discuss the issues.

The Discussion

"How's it going?" asked Bryan.

"Great," Gail said. "We've almost finished standardizing all the exhibit labels and are working on some new introductory panels. We have some great artifacts in the collection to use in mini-exhibitions about Burmilana County holiday celebrations. I have an appointment with the high school history teachers to discuss some collaborations."

"That's a lot of work in three months! How has the volunteer training been going?"

"Sometimes I feel like I should count to twenty. They are trying to help but get so agitated about change. I mean, the teenagers are fine. Once you get them to stop playing with their phones, they do what they are supposed to do. The others don't even want to change the labels with misspellings. The board wants me to professionalize the museum, but I'm the only professional. I'm working sixty hours a week and getting nothing done."

"The board isn't expecting you to revamp the entire museum in your first three months. You are supposed to be assessing the museum and creating a project plan to discuss at the quarterly review. You don't have to change anything right now."

"The misspelled labels drive me nuts."

"Ok, I'll give you that one. Remember how we also talked about how you would need to train the volunteers. You all have the same commitment and passion. They want the museum to be great. You have the advantage of a professional education that you now have to share with your colleagues who don't have that advantage. How are you teaching them to write labels?"

"I showed them the Serrell *Exhibit Labels* book and said they should use it to learn how to write labels. They submitted new versions that I reviewed. They were all unusable. So I had to completely redo them."

"Pointing to a book on a shelf isn't enough. You have to show examples of good labels and talk them through writing a label. You could brainstorm together. After they gave you their labels, you could have sat down together for constructive critiques. How else will they learn? How else will you be able to delegate tasks? Working sixty hour weeks will burn you out."

Gail sat silently.

Bryan said, "We need to talk about the holiday decorations. You know how important those decorations are to the community. The historical society depends on community good will and support."

Gail replied, "We have some amazing holiday artifacts in the collection, including historic photographs. We should be sharing those items, not chain store leprechauns."

"Why not do both? Over time, we can move the focus to the museum collection. We need to raise $30,000, so we need a happy community, not a pissed off community. These issues are going to come up at the board meeting. I want you to be prepared to answer the questions. You also have to present your assessment results and project plan. Why don't we review those now?"

After reviewing Gail's report, Gail and Bryan discussed volunteer management and prepared to answer board member concerns about the impact of Gail's actions on the volunteers and the historical society. At the board meeting, Gail should be prepared to answer the following questions:

1. Why did she disregard the board's instructions to focus on the project report during her first quarter?
2. What is her plan to train and manage the volunteers?
3. What other resources does Gail need to improve her management skills?

Other questions to consider:

1. Should board members have remained day-to-day site managers as Gail transitioned into her new role?
2. Was Gail hired as a director too early in her career?
3. Was it appropriate for Bryan to stress the dollar commitment needed from the community?

CASE 3: WILIS ART MUSEUM

Poor board recruitment was affecting membership renewals at the Wilis Art Museum. The community perceived board members as too old and too insular. A previous attempt at creating a junior board was unsuccessful. The board recognized the problem and created a subcommittee to create a new recruitment plan. Board members Ellen, Dorothy, and Charlie were selected for the subcommittee. Bill, the museum director, and Carrie, the director of development and membership, represented the museum on the committee.

Museum Background

The Wilis Art Museum had been a nationally recognized regional art museum in the 1950s and 1960s. The town of Wilis was located near several artist colonies. In 1952, several artists donated pieces to establish the Wilis Art Museum, in appreciation of the community's support of the art created in its environs.

The board was initially composed of four artists and eight members of the community. The artists provided expertise about the collection, and the community members guided the business decisions. Over time, the artist colonies moved to other regions. The board was now composed entirely of non-artists. A seat on the Wilis board had been considered the pinnacle of community service until the 1990s. Community leaders then began joining the boards of education and human services nonprofit organizations.

Community critics observed that the relatives and friends of board members were invited to join the board at a said board member's funeral. When Carrie reviewed member surveys, concerns about "cozy relationships" and "stodginess" were repeated. Membership renewals dropped 35 percent in the past year when an eighty-year-old board member convinced the rest of the board to appoint his eighty-three-year-old brother. Bill and Carrie had presented that information to the board at the previous meeting. All agreed that a new board recruitment plan was needed immediately. The subcommittee of Bill, Carrie, Ellen, Dorothy, and Charlie was established. Two seats were up for election in a few months. If new people were not nominated, the board knew that the community reaction would be disastrous.

The Museum Staff

Bill and Carrie had offered to review other museums' board recruitment strategies and to present their recommendations to the rest of the subcommittee. All five subcommittee members would then draft a plan for the board's review.

Bill was celebrating his tenth year as the Wilis museum director. Formerly the museum's curator, Bill's passion, business acumen, and collegiality impressed the board. When the previous director retired, the board agreed that Bill should be offered the position. Bill was a bit concerned about his lack of fundraising experience, especially in this time of waning community and government support. He loved the Wilis and decided to try to reignite the community's love for the museum.

Carrie joined the Wilis eight years ago. She had been the assistant development director at a large metropolitan art museum. The Wilis Art Museum was her first opportunity to run a development department. Her ultimate career goal was to head the development department at a large, internationally renowned museum. The Wilis' failure to meet her development goals frustrated her career plans. She was displeased that the board had backed away from her previous recruitment plans.

Bill and Carrie's Meeting

Carrie said, "We must try the junior board again."

Bill replied, "Our needs are more urgent. I don't want the discussion to devolve into another rehash of the past junior board experience. We have to focus on the main board."

Three years prior, Carrie had persuaded the board to create a junior board, who would supply technology and marketing expertise in the short term and would be groomed for the main board in the long term. The board agreed with the general goal, but expressed concern that the junior board members were not subject to the giving obligations of the main board. Bill and Carrie explained that educating the junior board members in board responsibilities would be part of the experience. Building a passion for the institution should be the priority; the financial support would follow. The board reluctantly agreed.

Carrie's insistence that each junior board member receive a free family membership during their first year on the junior board raised eyebrows. When Bill supported the idea, the board reluctantly agreed.

Unfortunately at the end of the first year, none of the junior board members renewed their family memberships or joined at other membership levels. Tony Stafford, an information technology (IT) professional, had helped the museum improve its website and convinced his brother, a local printer, to offer the museum a nonprofit discount. Tony's seventy-hour work week precluded further participation on the junior board.

Carrie said, "The junior board wasn't a total loss. We've saved thousands of dollars in printing costs. We could try again and require a family membership or a certain number of volunteer hours. Moms with kids would be happy to volunteer at the children's programs."

"You mean the annual children's program," Bill replied. "That's not enough. We should have reached out to the gallery owners."

"The three, poor gallery owners," interjected Carrie.

"Who are a base of people committed to the arts and know the local collectors," continued Bill. "I think we should reach out to the gallery owners, admit our predicament, and invite them to join the board. They have a better relationship with the collector community than we do and can help us craft a compelling pitch to eventually join the board or support the museum. Up to this point, frankly, we have failed."

After a few minutes of silence, Bill said, "I appreciate your hard work and willingness to reach out beyond the art community. We had to do that, and I supported those efforts. You were hired because you are a risk taker. Not all risks pay off. The junior board didn't work, so we have to move on to another strategy that is less risky and has an immediate payoff. I think half of the board would retire if they were confident in the slate of candidates. We need to find those candidates. Are you comfortable reaching out to the gallery owners?"

"Yeah," said Carrie.

"Ok, we'll share that strategy with Ellen, Dorothy, and Charlie," said Bill. "If we can recruit two or three viable candidates, membership should bounce back."

Carrie definitely wanted that membership rejuvenation. Her future career prospects depended on it.

The Board Strategy

"Does everyone have their Center for Non-Profit Management report?" asked Ellen.

"Yes," said Charlie. "Good thing we're not a ballet company."

Dorothy suppressed a laugh, while Ellen glared. Sensitive to criticism about its average age of seventy-five, the board prided itself on reading the current literature about nonprofit institutions, board best practices, and art museum issues. They attended BoardSource webinars. They were embarrassed at their inability to recruit younger community members to join the Wilis Art Museum board.

Dorothy said, "Ellen, we all know science, technology, engineering, and mathematics (STEM) education and climate change nonprofits are more important to young people. They want to help people. We need to explain how an art museum helps people. My son won't join our board because he doesn't think we help people."

"We help people appreciate art," replied Ellen.

"Meals on Wheels helps people eat. They win," said Charlie. "If we can show people how art is used to support political movements or memorialize human suffering, we might get one or two."

Charlie's bluntness was not appreciated by all the board members. His accurate assessments of situations and suggestions for viable solutions were, sometimes grudgingly, acknowledged.

"What about your neighbor?" asked Dorothy. "Isn't she a clay artist? She works with developmentally disabled kids. She could be great on the board."

Ellen replied, "Her husband might be transferred to Portland, so she doesn't want to commit. Can we at least agree to veto a junior board?"

"It was a good idea," said Dorothy. "It just didn't work out. Poor Carrie."

"If it had worked, she'd be gone," observed Charlie.

"Good riddance," said Ellen. We need people who are committed to the museum, like Bill."

"We need someone ambitious to prod us out of our laziness. We've been coasting on our reputation from the 1960s," retorted Charlie.

After a few more heated exchanges, Ellen, Dorothy, and Charlie tried to think of other community groups who supported local institutions and had past relationships with the Wilis Art Museum.

Dorothy read the list, "The Chamber of Commerce, the school board, the Arts Council, and the aldermen. We can informally approach each group, see who is most sympathetic, invite them to dinner, and see if they are willing to join our board."

"I don't want willing people," said Ellen. "I want passionate people."

"Ellen, we have to recognize that these people have other obligations. We can't expect them to spend forty hours a week working on board projects," said Dorothy. "We might have to expand the board or create another junior board. We need younger people. We can't afford to appoint any more eighty-year-olds."

"Exactly," said Charlie. "Fundraising hasn't taken a hit . . . yet. If we add one more old codger to the board, we'll all be spending eighty hours a week standing on the street with tin cups."

Charlie's words accurately represented the board's real concern about the future of the Wilis Art Museum.

The Subcommittee Meeting

"Carrie and I suggest a very targeted approach to the gallery owners, which will reestablish our presence within the local art community and also introduce us to local collectors," said Bill. "Convincing one or two gallery owners to join the board will also improve our credibility with the community at large."

"Just the gallery owners?" asked Ellen.

"Two board positions are open for election in the fall," replied Bill. "A natural time for change. If we can convince the gallery owners to join the board, then we can reach out to other community leaders for subsequent board elections."

"What about a junior board?" asked Ellen.

"We learned a lot from our previous junior board experiment. Our new printing contract has yielded significant savings. The issue at hand is the main board. If our success in recruiting people for the fall election generates a group of people who are interested in helping the museum, we can explore resurrecting the junior board," said Bill.

Dorothy then shared their list of candidate pools, kicking off a discussion of the merits of each group. The subsequent recommendation to the board must answer the following questions:

1. What are the two most viable board candidate pools? What are the merits and drawbacks of those pools?
2. What is the approach strategy?
3. What argument will convince people to regard the art museum as providing a service to the community?

Other questions to consider:

1. Is the subcommittee creating a strategy or a short-term solution to a long-term problem?
2. If the junior board is reconstructed, what changes, if any, should be implemented?
3. Are age limits appropriate for board members?

EPILOGUE

Communication is the core issue for all three of these case studies. If the Wilis Art Museum communicated more effectively with its community, its board member candidate pool would be larger. The Burmilana County Historical Society anticipated communication issues with its new museum director and planned accordingly, yet major communication problems still occurred. The Gerdes Children's Museum created a communication plan to help board members track their giving and now must decide if the plan should be formalized.

Even with the best of intentions, miscommunication will occur. The interpersonal relationships between the board members and the museum staff determine their ability to have a constructive dialogue. Disagreements about strategies and tactics are expected. Mutual respect and professionalism ensure a successful dynamic.

Chapter 2

Fundraising

INTRODUCTION

Every institution has its own unique fundraising needs and strategies. Some institutions may have difficulties simply raising funds, while others may have difficulties managing the expectations of donors of multimillion-dollar gifts. All institutions suffer when the fundraising strategy is unclear or ill-defined.

This chapter features three case studies exploring:

- staff needs and donor desires;
- fundraising strategies and tactics;
- planned needs and ad hoc needs; and
- the use of fundraising consultants.

In all these cases, the specific amount of money needed is fundamentally irrelevant. The real challenge is to understand your institution. As you develop solutions to the questions asked at the end of each case study, consider the impact of the staff, board, donors, and community on crafting a viable fundraising strategy.

CASE 1: LEWTON SCIENCE MUSEUM

The Lewton Science Museum began offering behind-the-scenes tours to members, VIPs, and school groups. Some of the taxidermy animals kept in curatorial storage contain arsenic from the old style of processing. To reduce the risk of harm, Phil Wronski, the natural history specimen curator, wants to remodel part of the storage space to relocate the arsenic animals to a restricted space. Jim Tolan, the museum director, agrees with Phil's proposal, which he then shares with two board members, Karen Welch and Kristina Nelson. Kristina regard the solution as too conservative. Phil's straightforward request balloons into a new wing for the museum.

Lewton Science Museum Background

The Lewton Science Museum was founded in 1922 by Gilbert Newton and Dana Lewis. Both men were acquaintances of Theodore Roosevelt and, like Teddy, enjoyed expeditions and hunting. Both men had worked on the Panama Canal and traveled to Africa, sending home plant and animal specimens that eventually became the core of the Lewton's collection.

In the Rooseveltian spirit of public service, Newton and Lewis decided to share their specimens with the public and created the Lewton. Since neither man came from wealthy families, they acquired a bankrupt buggy factory and turned it into a museum. Wealthy friends and a modest museum admission fee kept the doors open during the Great Depression.

Located in Dunston, a city with an average population of two hundred thousand, attendance from local citizens and school groups provided the Lewton with a steady attendance of eighty thousand per year. The reputation of its South American reptile collection grew from the 1960s, attracting scholars from around the world and enabling the Lewton to secure grants for various special projects.

The museum maintained a reputation for financial prudence and respected niche collections. The curatorial staff consisted of well-regarded scholars who balanced their own research with the needs of other researchers.

Over the years, the Lewton's board and staff took pride in its reputation for stability and scholarship. The budget always balanced, and its capital reserve fund always maintained twelve months of expenses. When the museum director retired in 2010, the board hired Jim Tolan, a tech savvy curator, who could help them create and implement a strategic plan for the twenty-first century.

Changes at the Lewton

The Lewton received positive reviews on Trip Advisor and museum comment cards. Visitors appreciated that the Lewton allowed photography and posted their pictures to social media accounts. The lack of interactive content, online educational materials for students, and the museum's own minimal social media presence were typical complaints. Jim was hired to resolve those issues.

Jim had been the curator at the Tinker Natural History Museum, an institution similar in size and mission to the Lewton. Jim's award-winning Omeka sites and Facebook presence intrigued the Lewton board. His popular Tinker behind-the-scenes tours had spurred memberships and donations. The Lewton soon experienced that success after Jim's hiring. He and the curatorial staff introduced the Behind the Brick Walls tours. The curatorial staff enjoyed sharing their favorite artifacts with visitors, as well as teaching people what curatorial work really entailed. They were also happy that Jim came from the curatorial world. The only issue was the arsenic animals.

Arsenic Animals

Arsenic was used in the taxidermy process from the nineteenth century until the 1970s. Like other natural history museums, the Lewton was testing its specimens for arsenic and was in the process of mounting the specimens in enclosed cases. As a precautionary measure, the curatorial staff assumed that all pre-1970s specimens were arsenic-positive until testing proved otherwise. Given the size of their collection, testing and mounting would take years. The staff continued working on the project.

Unfortunately, the specimen storage and work area was one large open space, with the specimens primarily stored on open shelving units. On tour days, the curatorial staff tried to sequester the arsenic animals, but visitors wandered and loved to touch specimens despite staff warnings. Phil, the curatorial director, was working on a plan to secure the specimen storage work area while still facilitating the Behind the Brick Walls tour (BBWs).

Phil's Plan

Phil and Jim met every two weeks to discuss key issues and to share preliminary thoughts about the monthly strategic planning meetings.

"I actually facepalmed myself," said Phil.

Jim laughed, "Why?"

"Because the solution to the arsenic problem is so obvious," said Phil. "In the public spaces, we subdivided the old factory floors to create individual galleries. We can do the same thing in our workspace. Janet and I measured the space. We could build a wall with a door thirty feet from the back door, which gives us egress for the fire code. We move some of the shelving units to that backroom. On the public-facing wall, we add shelves and display touchable items—direct that urge in a safe way. It should only cost between fifteen and twenty thousand. I can wait another year for the new scanners and software, so we can reallocate those funds. Janet and I will feel better knowing that the guests are safe." Janet was the assistant curator.

"You're right," Jim said. "The solution was too obvious. I like the shelving with touchables idea. I am concerned about sacrificing the scanners. Janet's big project for the year is digitizing the photos from the first Newton and Lewis Africa expedition."

"Unfortunately, we didn't win the grant, so we are paying for everything out of our budget. I understand that the board wants the photos digitized and posted online, but public safety comes first."

"Absolutely. Since the board is in favor of the BBWs and the digitization project, we might be able to secure some donations or special funding for both projects. I'm having lunch with Kristina and Karen tomorrow and can get their thoughts. We should be able to do both projects."

Jim and Phil discussed other business, confident that both projects would move forward.

The Board Member Lunch

Jim regularly had lunch with individual board members. Karen and Kristina were best of friends and preferred to lunch together. Both women had served on the board for nine years and would be leaving in a year due to term limits. They wanted their last year to be memorable.

"Attendance has been phenomenal this year," said Karen.

"That's why we need more computer terminals and those interactive games. Kids have short attention spans. They need to see something new every time they visit! We have to make the museum exciting," said Kristina.

"For all the technology," observed Jim, "we get the most comments and biggest crowds around the Frogs of the Amazon diorama."

"It's so boring," replied Kristina. "Could we at least add a TV screen and show a documentary about frogs?"

"I think we have enough TV screens," said Karen. "People love the BBWs because they see more real specimens. They're unique. We can all see documentaries at home on TV."

Jim said, "I'm glad you brought that up. Per the board's request, Phil has a solution to our arsenic animal problem. It's so simple. I'm kicking myself for not thinking of it. For fifteen or twenty thousand, we can just build a divider wall. Phil came up with a great idea to add shelves to the wall and put touchable specimens on the shelves. The only problem is that we would have to use the money currently allocated for the digitization project to stay on budget. We could also do a mini-fundraiser and do both projects. What are your initial thoughts?"

Although she usually spoke first, Kristina was strangely quiet. Karen waited a moment and then replied, "That's the perfect solution. Easy and obvious is sometimes too easy and obvious. The photos are probably the easier fundraising ask. We could divide them into groups and ask people to sponsor the elephants. I'm not sure people will be excited about building a wall."

"A wing," said Kristina.

"We only need a wall," said Karen.

"The real problem is that the museum staff and board think too small," replied Kristina. "We have enough land to build a wing with classrooms, a catering kitchen, and a theater. Then we can hold the annual fundraising dinner in the classrooms and ditch the restaurant. We can show nature films or host plays in the theater. Between the theater tickets and the event rental fees, the wing will pay for itself. I'll put up half the money for naming rights."

"Kristina," said Karen, "the museum doesn't need a theater or a catering kitchen. Where would we even find the brick to match the current building?"

"Buggies were obsolete when the museum began in that building," said Kristina. "We need a contemporary building. Other museums have added new wings to old buildings. Right, Jim?"

"Yes," replied Jim. "Those types of additions can be created thoughtfully to complement the existing structure. I have to say, your generosity is . . . overwhelming. We discussed some of those ideas during the strategic planning process. Other board members lacked your enthusiasm."

"Well, they're not on the board any more. I still am. A new wing will actually take the museum into the twenty-first century. Don't you agree?" said Kristina.

"A new wing with those features does provide us with additional tools to fulfill our mission," replied Jim. "We certainly need to do a cost-benefit analysis and think about all the possibilities for the space."

"This wing is happening," said Kristina. "So figure out how you want to use it."

"Kristina!" exclaimed Karen. "You don't know if the rest of the board will approve. The board opposed that idea when we created the five-year strategic plan. If we build this wing, we will have to rewrite the plan. It took us two years to write it."

"I'll pay for a consulting firm to write the new plan," said Kristina.

"That's not the point," said Karen. "The museum is executing the current plan. A new wing is too disruptive. Who's going to staff the kitchen? Are you going to pay for a cook? Are you going to buy pots and pans?"

Jim sat quietly as Karen and Kristina continued their discussion. He knew the museum lacked the staff to manage additional facility rentals, a classroom, and a theater. Maintaining all that new equipment would be expensive, too.

The old board was opposed to a new wing when Kristina proposed it. They didn't see the need and opposed the increased expenses. Since additional staff salaries were not included in the wing plan, Jim had publicly voted against the project. Privately, he wanted the wing.

Jim had been at the Lewton for six years. Unlike most of his museum director colleagues, he never worried about meeting fundraising goals and enjoyed low staff turnover. The Lewton was popular in its community and among tourists. The one flaw was the lack of a marquee project for his resume. Though Jim wasn't planning on leaving, he also understood the unpredictability of the museum world and updated his resume regularly. He knew that the staff would be concerned about the new construction, but successful risks could push the Lewton to a whole other level.

Jim Shares the News

Returning to the museum, Jim looked for Phil.

"I have great news," said Jim.

"We can have the wall and the digitization project," said Phil.

"Better," replied Jim. "We can have a new wing with classrooms, a catering kitchen, and a theater. We will have so many more opportunities for programs and events."

"Am I still getting my wall?"

"Sure."

"Are we still digitizing the photos?

"Absolutely."

"Will additional staff be hired for the wing?"

"Well, we haven't discussed all the details."

"So Kristina is getting her wing, and we're getting more work."

"Phil, you have to be willing to take risks. The museum has sound financials and a great staff. There's no reason to think that we can't extend that success. As a senior member of the staff, I expect your support and enthusiasm."

Phil pursed his lips and said, "No one should ever question my loyalty to the Lewton." He turned around and walked back to his office.

Jim felt a twinge of guilt about questioning Phil's loyalty. Well, he was really questioning Phil's risk tolerance. Staidness was a common concern about the Lewton. Jim did not want the staff to become complacent. The new wing would create more opportunities for all the departments to explore new ways to fulfill the mission.

When Kristina originally proposed a new wing, membership and donations had been flat. The BBW tours hadn't begun. The museum had fewer interactives. Now, membership and donations were growing. The new members expected the Lewton to continue creating new experiences. A new wing would provide even more excitement.

Jim began to work on his presentation to the board. That presentation must answer the following questions:

1. How will a new wing support the museum's mission?
2. Is the new wing fiscally responsible?
3. How will the wing be staffed?

Other questions to consider:

1. Should Jim keep the board focused on solving the original problem, the arsenic animals? Why or why not?
2. If the board has already created a five-year strategic plan and vetoed/ approved specific initiatives, should a museum director or board member use board seat changes to reopen those discussions?
3. How should museums balance risk and financial responsibility?

CASE 2: PUTNAM ART MUSEUM

The Putnam Art Museum's annual gala is renowned for its lavish spending and lavish donations. The gala is the main fundraiser and public relations event each year. Three years ago, board member Julie Sewall became the gala chairwoman. Socially connected and renowned for her own private parties, Julie appeared to be an excellent choice. Julie's extravagant spending and snubbing of in-kind donors has translated into diminishing returns for the museum. Betty Todd, the museum's director of development, wants to replace Julie and must convince Lisa Peterson, the museum director, and Mark Hayes, the board chair, that Julie is harming the Putnam's fundraising.

Putnam Art Museum Background

Officially founded in 1846, the Putnam Art Museum began life a century and a half prior as a showroom for the goods imported into Putnam, a New England seaport. Merchants and wealthy families visited that showroom to inspect samples and place orders. As the sea trade declined, interest in viewing the jade, porcelain, and silks remained. Art and history scholars used the collection to study trade routes and the evolution of art movements. Supported by local wealthy families, the showroom became the Putnam Art Museum. Works from local artists were added to the collection. Its archives contained the papers of statesmen and writers.

The Putnam's ten million dollar annual budget was high for a museum of its square footage, but accurately reflected the costs of facilitating public access to and preserving the collection. Special projects, like the new website for the Samuel Jade Collection, were funded by grants. The annual gala was the cornerstone of the museum's fundraising activities.

The annual gala was launched in 1953 after the museum acquired a collection of maritime engravings. That first gala celebrated that acquisition and raised funds for conservation work on the engravings. Its continued success has been celebrated and studied by other museum professionals. Over the years, the gala contributed 1–5 percent of the museum's budget. Potential board members and donors were cultivated. Current donors were thanked. Upcoming exhibits and educational programs were showcased. Scholars who had used the collection were invited to share their work. Local, regional, and national press covered the event. Chair of the gala was considered a plum assignment by the board.

Julie Sewall, a vivacious and popular board member, seemed the perfect choice for chair of the gala. Her personal parties were the highlight of every social season, and Julie had persuaded several businesses to donate to the museum. Julie's enthusiasm and dedication were unquestioned. Betty, the museum's director of development, was beginning to question Julie's financial management skills.

Crunching the Numbers

As gala season approached, Betty reviewed the financial statements from the past five years and prepared the board summary (see Table 2.1).

The trends troubled her. Julie became the chair of the gala three years ago. She was able to inspire donors to increase their gifts. Her relationships with the in-kind gala donors were rockier. Betty had previously managed the in-kind donations for the gala, freeing the chair to focus on grooming cash donors and potential board members. Julie persuaded the board to let her manage the in-kind donations, too.

Julie had assumed that she could just as easily persuade the vendors to donate their best champagne or red rose and Swarovski centerpieces. The vendors did regard the gala as an excellent opportunity to showcase their goods and services to high-end potential customers, but also had to be financially responsible to their own businesses. Julie wanted the best and paid a premium for her personal parties. She expected that the vendors would respect her personal spending and be grateful for the opportunity to work at the gala gratis. Betty had usually purchased a few items and worked with the vendors to select donated items that met gala standards and were financially reasonable for the vendors.

Perturbed with uncooperative vendors, Julie switched vendors and did not ask the new vendors for in-kind donations. She used museum funds to pay the

Table 2.1 Putnam Art Museum Gala Fundraising Board Summary

	Year One	Year Two	Year Three	Year Four	Year Five
Total Donations (Cash and In-Kind)	200,000	250,000	300,000	450,000	500,000
Total Expenses	100,000	100,000	225,000	280,000	340,000
Net	100,000	150,000	75,000	170,000	160,000

vendors, with the board's approval. When Betty asked if Julie would consider paying for the new vendors as part of Julie's annual giving requirement, Julie became indignant and persuaded the board that the museum should pay the cost. Julie's galas did raise more money than past galas, so the board was willing to overlook the increased expenses.

Betty knew that the rising expenses were not sustainable in the long term. She was able to salvage the relationships with the previous gala vendors by using them for other museum programs and still receiving in-kind donations. She also knew that those vendors were still bitter about their ouster and had lost other customers. Betty was sure that she could use the new financial statements to persuade the board to replace Julie and to welcome back the old vendors.

Lisa and Mark Meet

Per the board's bylaws, the chair of the gala was officially selected each year. The museum director, the board chair, and the director of development reviewed the previous gala's financial statement and drafted a recommendation to the board. The previous year's chair of the gala was either reinvited to serve or replaced. In practice, the chair of the gala remained until they decided to resign. The board had never "dismissed" a chair of the gala.

Lisa, the museum director, and Mark, the board chair, anticipated reinviting Julie, despite Betty's qualms.

"I still can't believe we had a half million dollars in donations last year," said Mark. "Julie really charmed those defense contractors."

"Jeff was very interested in the board," said Lisa. "His undergrad minor in art history was a surprise. I've never known anyone with a math major and art history minor. He signed up for a family membership. His kids have been coming to the Maritime Monday programs. He could really help us craft our art and STEM arguments. We have some grant applications coming up and could really use his perspective."

"Did you talk to the boat builder?" asked Mark. "He doesn't have any money but was interested in collaborating on a program or educational activity. He has a lot of charisma and would be great on TV."

"Yeah, we need more camera-ready people for web videos. We could do a whole series on boat building—if we can get a grant. For the board agenda, we need to discuss the Thornehill manuscript collection. The pages are deteriorating faster than we estimated, so we will need to increase that budget next year. It'll probably be cheaper to buy some of that equipment. If Roger can work with the preservation team again, that would be great."

Roger was a board member, who was also a CFO at a manufacturing company. His skill at crafting understandable cost–benefit analyses was legendary. His forecasts were always accurate, within the margin of error.

"Do you think we should have Roger review the gala financials?" asked Mark.

Lisa laughed.

"I'm serious," said Mark. "The tension between Julie and Betty is affecting all of our development efforts. Both are excellent, and I don't want to lose either. They need to coexist."

"I agree," said Lisa. "Now is the opportunity for the board to review the numbers and affirm or reject Julie's approach. I share Betty's concerns about the vendor relationships and increasing costs. Julie has brought people like Jeff to the gala. She knows everyone and makes people feel part of the group—even if they are new. Maybe Roger can figure out a way to quantify Julie's people skills."

"Let's call him now," said Mark.

Roger's Input and Betty's Calculations

Lisa and Mark called Roger to ask his advice.

"Oh, that's interesting," said Roger. "I calculate goodwill, brand value, and other intangibles. In terms of people, at the end of the day, everyone is replaceable—from a finance point of view. Hmmm, we have several years' worth of data and could develop some type of coefficient. Yes, this could be very interesting. I need to do some research. See if anybody else has tried."

"Don't start yet," said Mark. "Lisa and I just needed to know if such a study was possible. Betty is presenting some numbers this afternoon, so we may not need to do anything. It's good to know that you can do it."

"Oh, yeah," said Roger. "I'm all over it."

"We appreciate your enthusiasm," said Lisa.

After finishing their conversation with Roger, Lisa and Mark reviewed other museum business while waiting for Betty's arrival. Both were confident that a data-driven solution could be reached. After Betty entered and gave them her worksheet, the three began their discussion.

"This new summary sheet is great, Betty," said Mark. "Seeing the totals for donations and expenses with the net gives the board a simple summary of the gala. Much better than wading through multiple spreadsheets to figure out how we did."

"Thank you," said Betty. "The gala is the lynchpin of our fundraising. Its outcome really sets the tone for the rest of the year."

"It does," said Lisa. "Both Mark and I share your concern about the increase in expenses, though we are excited to see the increase in cash donations. We also appreciate how you have maintained the relationships with our veteran in-kind donators."

"Your relationship skills are terrific," said Mark.

"Ok," said Betty. "What's up? This is starting to feel like you are softening me up for bad news."

"We all know about the tension between you and Julie. You are both very professional, but you both have different philosophies about managing the gala," said Mark.

"Correct," said Betty.

"To be fair," continued Mark. "Lisa and I are going to recommend that Roger create some type of fiscal analysis using your data and quantifying Julie to assess the gala. Once we have that information, the board can decide what to do."

"How are you going to quantify Julie?" asked Betty.

"Roger thinks he can do it," said Lisa.

"Are you going to quantify me?" asked Betty.

"We hadn't thought about that," said Lisa. "We can certainly ask him."

"I think that would be fair," said Betty. "We both have different skills and responsibilities. I would feel more comfortable with the board studying and then selecting a gala fundraising philosophy. Then my team can work effectively with Julie."

"We absolutely want to be fair," said Lisa. "We also need to know if the gala is still successful."

Betty, Mark, and Lisa continued reviewing the financials and logistics and preparing information for the board and Roger. Each person wondered about the board's reaction and prepared to answer the following questions:

1. Are in-kind donations critical to the success of the gala?
2. How will Roger's study help the board decide between Betty's and Julie's strategies?
3. Does the income increase more than offset the increase in expenses?

Other questions to consider:

1. Given their inherent costs, are galas a cost-effective fundraising activity?
2. Should the board or the museum development staff drive the tactical fundraising decisions?
3. What criteria should a museum use to discontinue a fundraising activity?

CASE 3: CAMERON HISTORY MUSEUM

Faced with an aging HVAC (heating, ventilation and air conditioning) system and poorly insulated windows, the Cameron History Museum has decided to mount its first capital campaign. The one hundred thousand dollars needed equals the museum's annual budget. Nora Adams, the museum's part-time development director, knows that she will need help creating and implementing a fundraising plan. She and Marilyn Byrd, the museum director, must present a plan to the museum board. Nora is willing to grow her skills, but Marilyn has a lot of doubts. Both women think a consultant will be helpful, but differ on the consultant's duties.

Cameron History Museum Background

The Cameron History Museum, founded in 1898, was located in Stoneridge, a rust-belt city whose fortune was rebounding but would probably never return to their post–World War II heights. Henry Cameron, the museum's founder, had also founded the city's newspaper. The museum had the complete run of the paper, some old printing presses, and the glass plate negatives of the early newspaper photos. The local genealogy society comprised half of the museum's membership and one-third of its visitors. Social studies students were another third, with other local citizens and tourist as the final third. The museum averaged five thousand visitors per year.

Housed in a Victorian home, the Cameron underwent annual inspections per city code. During the last inspection, the city official was concerned that the HVAC system was reaching the end of its natural life. He suggested that the museum replace the system within a few years and install energy efficient windows to lower the electric bill. The museum board and staff recognized that those improvements would also support their conservation plans.

The museum had three part-time employees: Marilyn, the museum director, Nora, the development and volunteer coordinator, and Kate, the curator and education coordinator. The board relied on Marilyn and Nora to draft recommendations and prioritize options. Everyone knew that the new windows and HVAC systems required raising more money than the museum ever had.

Nora was an accountant and financial planner. She kept the museum's books and managed its small endowment. Membership fees, admission, gift shop sales, photocopy fees, the annual picnic fundraiser, donations, and endowment interest covered the annual budget. When the museum needed new equipment, people either donated the item or participated in a special fundraiser. The last special fundraiser had generated ten thousand dollars for computers, scanners, and software.

When Nora realized how much money would be needed for this campaign, she was worried. She did not have any experience in creating and managing such a large campaign. The board hired her for her accounting skills. No one had thought that the museum would need to raise six figures. Nora decided to embrace the challenge.

She had a good relationship with the owner of the local appliance store. She might be able to get a discount or an in-kind donation, but would still need a lot of money. She reread her copy of *Fundraising for Small Museums* and tried to write a case statement. She quickly felt overwhelmed. The museum didn't have key donors. Board members had limited financial resources. Nora wasn't even sure if the campaign was feasible. She decided to meet with Marilyn and discuss the possibility of hiring a fundraising consultant.

Marilyn's Research

Marilyn was very concerned about the fundraising challenge. Nora was incredibly diligent and hardworking, but she was also shy. Marilyn recognized her own limitations, too. Terrified of public speaking, Marilyn rehearsed her presentations for hours. Her husband, Ken, a pharmaceutical sales representative, gave her pointers and helped her network with people at the annual picnic. Though Ken agreed to help with this new fundraising campaign, his work travel schedule kept him on the road most of the week.

Thinking about the board, Marilyn knew that none of them could afford to give more than their existing board giving requirement. In her museum management class, she had learned that best practice was to raise 50 percent of the money before starting construction. Even Ken was unable to convince the wealthy families in town to give one hundred dollars to the Cameron. They told him that the animal shelter and free health clinic were worthier recipients of their dollars.

"You don't need them," said Ken. "You can raise the money in smaller chunks. Who cares if one person gives one thousand dollars or one hundred people give ten dollars? It's all cash."

"Ten dollars at a time will take forever," said Marilyn. "Nora, Kate, and I are part-time at the museum and at other jobs. We could barely pull together that grant application for children's programs."

"You did pull it together, and you got the grant. Everyone in town was impressed. That was front page news. Ride that momentum to one hundred thousand dollars."

"What are we going to do, a bake sale every week? A car wash every week?"

"Can you access the principal from the endowment?"

"That was done in 1975 to rebuild the foundation. Although everyone agreed it was within the by-laws, the museum director and board were all replaced within two years."

"Ouch! Well, all you really need is a schmoozer. Can't you just hire someone to work the crowd?"

"I doubt we could afford anyone good or reputable."

"Pay them on commission. Sales people work on commission all the time. Problem solved."

Marilyn thought about Ken's suggestion and decided to reach out to some of her fellow museum directors. Hopefully, one of them would know a good fundraiser.

Considering the Options

Nora said, "I think it will be tough. If we give ourselves twenty-four months, I think we can do it. The Grace brothers are willing to give us as much equipment at cost as they can. We could be okay raising just seventy-five thousand. I think we should hire very experienced workers and make sure everything is done right the first time. I have a draft of a case statement. We can edit it. I think it gives us a start."

"You've been working hard," said Marilyn. "I'm nervous. None of us have ever done anything like this."

"Yes," sighed Nora. "I really think we should hire a fundraising consultant to help us refine our plan."

"Actually, I think we should hire a fundraiser to handle the entire process," said Marilyn.

Nora sat quietly.

"I mean none of us are experienced. Even if our intentions are good, we could screw up and never get the money," said Marilyn.

"We can try," said Nora. "I don't think people will want to give money to an outsider. It's our responsibility to do the work. The Foundation Center has free online training and tutorials. We can draft our materials and have a consultant review that work. We don't have any money to pay for someone to manage the entire process."

"We can hire a fundraiser on commission."

"No!"

Marilyn was startled by Nora's adamant response.

"The Association of Fundraising Professionals Code of Ethics prohibits commission-based payments. At the very least, we should pay someone a base salary and then maybe tiered incentives. This person needs time to build a plan and a donor base from scratch," argued Nora.

"So if we pay the person a base salary, you would support the idea?" asked Marilyn.

"There's no money to pay someone a salary. We can probably afford five hundred dollars for a consultant. We need to do as much of prep work as we can, so the person can focus on the core issues and edit our work."

"We don't know what we are doing. Yeah, we can read a book and watch a webinar, but we need real experience."

"It's our own fault that we don't have experience. We knew that we would have to replace the windows and HVAC eventually. We should have started a capital campaign five years ago. I'm sorry to be so blunt, and I accept the lion's share of the responsibility. That's why I want to step up and make this work. I've really thought about this. I think we aren't respected because we are too timid. People will give us money if we are confident."

"We still need a lot of money. If we make a mistake, the town will remember."

"Yeah, but over one hundred thousand people live here. We know most of them don't visit the museum and don't know anything about us. The genealogy society has more members than we do. They are always raising money for their indexing projects. The public library just raised twenty-five thousand dollars to redo the children's department. We should ask them for help."

"I just think it'll be easier to hire a professional fundraiser. I don't understand the ethical issue," said Marilyn.

"Someone working on pure commission is incentivized to extract all of the money possible without thinking about future giving. Some donors may not want to give because they want the museum to get all the money."

"If we are paying a consultant or hiring a temporary fundraiser, they're taking money from the institution, too," replied Marilyn. "We should pay for the greater chance at success."

"What did the other museum directors say?" asked Nora.

"Some of them have personal connections who can give big donations and get the ball rolling. Others are just good at raising money. Nobody else has used a consultant."

"What do you want to tell the board? Aren't we supposed to give them one recommendation?"

"We are," said Marilyn. "I think we both have strong arguments and passion for our positions. The board will be better served if we both present our individual recommendations. Then they can make an informed decision."

"They usually do what you tell them."

"I usually present a consensus position. I don't think we can reconcile our recommendations, so the board will have to."

Marilyn and Nora left their meeting to draft their board presentations. Neither knew how the board would react to their recommendations. Each was firmly convinced that her plan was best for the museum. To persuade the board, both had to answer the following questions:

1. Is hiring a fundraising consultant or a fundraiser the more effective choice? Why?
2. Since the HVAC system and windows do not need to be immediately replaced, what are the repercussions if the board delays consideration of the issue?
3. Should the museum contact other institutions, like the genealogy society, for help?

Other questions to consider:

1. Is commission-based compensation for a fundraiser ethical? Why or why not?
2. Are capital reserve funds essential for every museum?
3. What professional development activities should be instituted to continually update staff skills?

EPILOGUE

An understanding of the institution is the core issue for all three case studies. The Lewton Science Museum has a strategic plan and two specific fundraising projects that could be derailed due to the desires of one board member. The Putnam Art Museum is successfully increasing its donations, but the board must explicitly affirm or deny the accompanying increase in expenses. The Cameron History Museum faces its first significant fundraising challenge with an inexperienced staff and limited resources.

The responsibilities of the board versus the museum staff and the strategies and tactics of the fundraising plan must be understood before a campaign begins. Both the board and the staff should continually hone their fundraising skills or utilize the services of a fundraising professional to maximize the success of a campaign.

Chapter 3

Personnel Management

INTRODUCTION

The skills, talents, ambitions, and personalities of a staff shape how an institution carries out its mission. A creative and charismatic director may support innovative programming and attract large donations. A passionate volunteer corps may provide an amazing visitor experience. Staff management skills are essential for a well-run museum, but do take time to learn.

This chapter features three case studies exploring:

- volunteer/staff recruitment;
- volunteer/staff dismissal;
- staff reduction; and
- the tension between personal ambitions and the good of the institution.

In all of these cases, individual personalities shape the reactions and interactions among the people involved. Managing personal emotions can be the real challenge in personnel management. As you develop solutions to the questions asked at the end of each case study, consider how your emotional reactions to the people are affecting your answers and which people are similar or dissimilar to you.

CASE 1: JAMES BENJAMIN HOUSE MUSEUM

The James Benjamin House Museum has three part-time employees: Alice Wagner, the museum director, Dolores Clark, the guest services/education manager, and Jill Harrison, the curator. Volunteers lead the tours, assist in conservation, and help with other museum operations. Longtime volunteer Mary Ellen Elston has been reprimanded several times for violating the policies in the volunteer handbook. She recently refused to admit a group of museum professionals who had arrived ten minutes early for a special tour. Dolores wants to fire Mary Ellen. Alice is reluctant due to Mary Ellen's standing in the community.

James Benjamin House Museum Background

In 1842, James Benjamin drove his covered wagon from the East Coast to the Midwestern prairie. He founded the town of Sterling, named for his mother's family. His wealth came from real estate, and his fame came from his political career. His house was the most opulent and technologically advanced manse of 1858. Upon his death in 1900, his heirs left Sterling for larger cities and gave the home to the town.

Through most of the twentieth century, Sterling schoolchildren visited the Benjamin House to complete their local history study unit. The house was eventually supplanted by the 1920s mansion of a local industrialist. The staff tried to create compelling educational materials for the local school, but lacked the staff and funding of its rival.

From Sterling's population of twenty-five thousand, the Benjamin received approximately two thousand visitors per year. The woodwork and hand-carved furniture were the primary attractions. The twenty thousand dollar annual budget was generated from town council funds, a state appropriation, admission fees, gift shop sales, and donations. The three part-time staff were originally volunteers. In recognition of their work to revitalize the Benjamin House, the board voted to hire Alice, Dolores, and Jill as part-time staff. The three women would have continued as volunteers, but appreciated the board's thoughtful recognition.

Revitalizing the Benjamin

Alice had managed a local nonprofit agency and began volunteering at the Benjamin upon her retirement. Dolores was a schoolteacher, and Jill was an artist. Each person had a special memory of the Benjamin from her youth and wanted to ensure the house's survival for another century. Alice was crafting a financial plan and had begun a small fundraising campaign. Dolores was updating the educational and tour materials. Jill was assessing the condition of the house and the collection. Another ten people were volunteers.

Mary Ellen had volunteered at the Benjamin for twenty years—longer than anyone else. Her family, the Elstons, was prominent, but no longer wealthy. "Irascible" was the word commonly used to describe Mary Ellen. Tart-tongued, she offended everyone who knew her at some point in time. That was her way. She was also hardworking and conscientious. Her loyalty was to the house itself, not to the board or her fellow volunteers. When the scion of the wealthiest family in town broke several artifacts in the house, Mary Ellen made the father pay for the repairs and donate new windows. She knew every inch of the house and every factual detail about James Benjamin. Her job was to impart those facts to visitors.

Mary Ellen expected people to pay attention during her tours and was known to "nudge" people with her cane to keep them moving. Tours began every hour on the hour, and the front door was opened five minutes prior. If you arrived early, you stood on the porch or could wait in the barn where you had paid your admission fee, regardless of weather. Most visitors experienced a Mary Ellen moment during their tour—to either their delight or chagrin.

The Volunteer Handbook

While some visitors were amused by Mary Ellen's crowd control techniques, others were not. After several complaints about the cane, the board told Mary Ellen to stop using it to nudge people. At that time, the Benjamin did not have a volunteer handbook. When Dolores was promoted to a part-time employee, the board asked her to create a handbook. She reviewed the *Standards and Best Practices for Museum Volunteer Programs*, published by the American Association for Museum Volunteers, and other museums' handbooks. Dolores defined the roles of the volunteers, policies, procedures, expectations, ethics, and techniques for interacting with visitors. She also drafted a volunteer application. The board approved the documents and grandfathered the current volunteers, as long as they signed and agreed to abide by the new handbook.

Mary Ellen signed the handbook and thought it would help keep the younger volunteers in check. No one needs to look at their phones every five minutes. Watches tell time, not phones.

The Incident

Dolores and Jill had offered to open the Benjamin House an hour early to provide a special tour for museum professionals attending the annual state museum conference in a nearby town. If the other museum professionals enjoyed their tour, they might agree to display Benjamin House rack cards at their sites. Dolores and Jill had also scheduled future special tours with an association of woodworkers. Their goal was to target specific groups who could have a special interest in the Benjamin and to forge deep relationships with those groups. They hoped that their fellow museum professionals might offer suggestions or hints after seeing the museum.

Dolores was supposed to lead the tour, but fell ill at the last minute. Jill was out of town, and Alice was attending a museum director's brunch at the conference. Mary Ellen was the only volunteer available. Dolores explained the importance of the group visit to Mary Ellen, who understood and wanted the museum to thrive.

The day of the tour was sunny and hot. The group was supposed to arrive at 9:50. The bus driver knew a short cut and arrived at 9:30. Assembling on the porch, one person rang the doorbell. When no one answered, the group wasn't surprised and prepared to spend time on the porch. A few minutes later, someone saw Mary Ellen inside the house and rang the bell again.

Mary Ellen answered the door, "You're too early."

"Yes," said the group leader. "We're sorry. We don't want to interrupt you while you are setting up for the tour. It's so hot out. Could we come inside and stay in the hallway?"

"No," said Mary Ellen. "Doors open five minutes before the start of the tour. Until then, you stay on the porch."

She closed the door, set up for the tour, and reopened the doors at 9:55. Attendees who had similar issues with volunteers were unsurprised. Other tour attendees were upset and shared their consternation with other conference participants, including Alice.

The Aftermath

Dolores was mortified when she learned about the incident and contacted each tour member to apologize. She also discussed the situation with Mary Ellen.

"I'm really surprised at what happened," said Dolores.

"They came early. We don't let people in early," said Mary Ellen.

"Typically no. But regular visitors can stay in the barn until the tour starts. The barn was closed, so you could have let them stay in the front hall to get out of the sun. They're museum professionals. They know how to behave."

Mary Ellen snorted, "Right, like the museum director who broke the closet door because he wanted to see if we piped HVAC through the closets, or the one who went through the desk drawers looking for family items. Museum people can be the worst guests."

"We can't let those experiences excuse what happened. You knew how important that visit was. We needed to form friendly relationships and promote the museum."

"I've been working at the museum longer than any of you. The Elston family has supported this museum for over a hundred years."

"We appreciate that. We are all trying to support and protect the museum. Now, we need more help, especially from people outside our community."

"If you want to change the rules, then change the rules. I follow the rules. We open the doors five minutes before tours start. I have to go give a tour now."

Firing a Volunteer

Dolores shared their conversation with Jill and Alice at their weekly meeting.

"Wow," said Jill. "She is technically right, but wrong. She knew this was a special situation. We do encourage the volunteers to use common sense and to prioritize guest comfort."

"When Mary Ellen gets nervous, she defaults to rules," said Alice. "She may have felt pressure because this visit was so important to the museum. She really does love the museum."

Dolores replied, "She may love the museum, but she is becoming a huge problem. People in our community may know and excuse her behavior, but out of town guests won't. What happens if people start posting negative comments online? We have so few visitors. We have to put our best foot forward."

"Her family has supported the museum for a long time. The Elston name has weight in the community," said Alice.

"They don't give money. They aren't on the board. They aren't the leaders that they were. How are they going to hurt us if we dismiss Mary Ellen?" asked Dolores.

"I agree with Dolores," said Jill. "Forty years ago, the Elstons were powerful community leaders. Most of them have moved out of town. The remaining family members really don't do anything. Half the town doesn't know who they are any more."

"The other half does," argued Alice. "We need to consider all the ramifications. We might lose a donor."

"Alice, three volunteers have already quit because of Mary Ellen. We're not upholding the standards of the volunteer handbook. When they sign the volunteer agreement, they are committing to following staff direction and to ensuring the safety and comfort of guests. Mary Ellen violated the agreement," said Dolores.

"I overheard a couple volunteers talking. They think that we are going to ignore the problem again. They think that we don't have the backbone to dismiss Mary Ellen and move the museum forward," said Jill. "I think more people will quit, and we will lose community support if we don't dismiss her."

Alice sighed and admitted, "The board has told me that we can dismiss Mary Ellen if we think she is hurting the museum. It's a tough decision. She is an institution."

"But is she hurting us more than she is helping us?" asked Jill.

The women decided that dismissing Mary Ellen was in the best interest of the museum. Alice asked that they all sleep on the decision and reconvene the next day to formalize the decision. Then they would notify Mary Ellen. To finalize the decision, the staff must answer the following questions:

1. Did Mary Ellen violate the volunteer agreement? If so, should Mary Ellen be dismissed? Why or why not?
2. Given her community standing, could Mary Ellen be offered a back of house role?
3. How will the dismissal impact the other volunteers?

Other questions to consider:

1. Should a volunteer automatically be dismissed for violating the volunteer agreement? Why or why not?
2. How should an institution balance its volunteer agreement requirements and the reputation or connection of specific volunteers?
3. If a museum lacks a volunteer handbook and agreement, how should it manage volunteers?

CASE 2: THE COPPERFIELD BOTANICAL GARDEN

The Copperfield Botanical Garden is increasingly criticized for a perceived elitism by the local press, which has negatively impacted attendance. The crux of the issue is the homogeneity of the volunteer corps: white people over the age of fifty. The board is pressuring June Piedmont the museum director, to diversify the volunteer pool. June is tasking Rhonda Gabler, the volunteer coordinator, and Hannah Simon, the education coordinator, with developing new volunteer recruitment strategies.

Copperfield Botanical Garden Background

Inhabiting one hundred acres, the Copperfield Botanical Garden was originally the estate of an Englishman who made and lost a fortune. Mr. Copperfield also lost the fortunes of other locals. In an attempt to reduce his prison sentence, he agreed to deed his land to the city of Woodstock. The land contained a house, barn, English-style garden, rose garden, and prairieland. The original intent was to resell the land, but the townspeople enjoyed the gardens and pressured the city to turn the estate into a public garden. The Copperfield Botanical Garden officially opened in 1933. Some people thought it should be named the Woodstock Botanical Garden, but others who were still sympathetic to the charming Mr. Copperfield prevailed.

As Woodstock recovered from the Great Depression, the city's population settled at two hundred fifty thousand. People enjoyed attending outdoor concerts and seasonal activities at the Copperfield. Visitation averaged sixty thousand people per year. The Copperfield had successfully established corporate sponsorships with national seed and garden supply companies. It secured grants for its annual summer camp for disadvantaged youth. Visitors from around the world came to see topiaries and rose varieties. The community was proud of the Copperfield.

The Expose

Mike Adams from *Channel 4 News* was the local investigative reporter who eagerly sought scandal. He probed every public or nonprofit institution in town. Though Adams sometimes sensationalized small issues, the citizenry did think that he kept officials on their toes. Adams also received tips before other members of the press.

June Piedmont, the museum director, learned that Adams was investigating the Copperfield. She presumed that the investigation might involve relationships with corporate sponsors, the budget for the annual gala, the failed outdoor movie program, or an issue with the Copperfield's sustainability policies. Instead, Adams criticized the Copperfield for its "elitist" volunteer corps.

June and the board immediately gave interviews to emphasize that the Copperfield invited all community members to volunteer or to enjoy the many programs, free and ticketed. When the city newspaper wrote a follow-up story, it noted that the volunteer corps was mainly composed of white people over the age of fifty, and that the staff and board demographics also did not reflect the ethnic and racial diversity of Woodstock.

The board decided to review its recruitment policy to emphasize the importance of the board reflecting its community. June was asked to review museum staff and volunteer recruitment policies.

June Meets with Rhonda and Hannah

June called a special meeting with Rhonda, the volunteer coordinator, and Hannah, the education coordinator, to discuss the board's assignment.

"Kate and I will be reviewing the staff recruitment policies and methodologies. We have identified a couple of job fairs that will introduce the Copperfield to a new group of people. We currently don't have any open positions, and I don't anticipate creating any new positions over the next year. The volunteer corps is where we can show an immediate change," said June.

"You do realize that we can't control who volunteers," said Rhonda.

"Yes," said June, "but we have to show that we understand the perception and are reaching out to everyone."

"Well, we really don't reach out to anyone now," said Hannah. "We just post a note in the break room and on the website. Maybe we should put more thought into it."

"I would be happy to do that," said Rhonda. "Unfortunately, the board did not approve my request for scheduling software. Organizing fifty people using a spreadsheet takes a while."

"Now you and Hannah can brainstorm together," said June. "We can try again next year for the scheduling software. I need a plan by next Tuesday. I have a TV interview next Friday and want to announce the new plan."

"Um, okay," said Hannah, while Rhonda glared.

"I look forward to your recommendation," said June as she left.

After some salty language, Rhonda and Hannah agreed to individually research volunteer recruitment tactics and reconvene the next day.

Rhonda and Hannah Strategize

Rhonda had worked at the Copperfield for fifteen years. She worked hard, and everyone admired her ability to manage the logistics of the fifty-person volunteer corps. Because she could do so much with so little, her requests were usually chopped first during budget season. The education coordinator position was Hannah's first professional position after receiving her master's degree. As the youngest member of the staff, Hannah was keenly aware of the Copperfield's diversity issues.

The two women had a strong working relationship and constructively challenged one another, which was June's primary reason for asking them to work on the plan. Hannah also needed more volunteers for her new education programs, so her input was critical.

The Copperfield used volunteers as docents, greeters, and administrative support. For liability reasons, volunteers were not used to maintain the gardens. Since the goal was to more accurately represent the community, Rhonda and Hannah decided to focus on local resources that could connect them with diverse groups of people.

"We naturally attract retired people because they have more time. They're older, so we need to attract younger people, though we do attract women who are five months pregnant for some reason. But they never come back after they have the baby," said Rhonda.

"I know. It's so strange," said Hannah. "Newborns do keep you busy."

"And sleep deprived."

"Maybe we should think about both the community and our visitors. Our biggest group of international visitors comes from Japan. A Japanese speaking docent would be great. We could also see if some of our campers are interested in becoming volunteers."

"That's actually a good idea," said Rhonda. "We have a booth at the county fair this year. We could include volunteer materials."

"Doesn't the fair attract the same type of people who already volunteer here?"

"I'm just trying to think of places that attract large groups of people."

"I think we should be more targeted. Think of skills we need and reach out to that community."

"That could be tricky."

"Woodstock has mostly people between ten and fifty, with significant Asian, Hispanic, and African-American communities. The summer campers reflect those ethnic and racial communities. We always need more peer counselors for the campers and haven't really done a good job asking former campers for help. We really do need Japanese and Chinese speaking docents for our international visitors. We could talk to their community centers."

"What about the other groups?" asked Rhonda.

"That is trickier," said Hannah. "But not impossible. Don't we have a Day of the Dead program planned?"

"Yes, but something bothers me about using ethnic programs for these purposes. Are we stereotyping or cultural appropriating? It seems very opportunistic."

"Yeah, I want everyone to feel welcome, but I don't want to force people to come either. The community college has diversity job fairs. Groups that need volunteers can also get booths. I think we need to go where people are, not wait for people to come to us."

"I agree," said Rhonda. "We get the same type of volunteers because we don't really recruit for skills or anything else. Our current volunteers recruit their friends, which is helpful. We have a great group of people. Honestly, I don't think most of our volunteers could help you with nature hikes or Judy with the Facebook page."

"I actually think Adams's expose was really helpful. Otherwise, we never would have the support to expand volunteer recruitment. I know it sucks for you, but I can help."

"Thanks, Hannah. Let's write down our suggestions and create an action plan."

Hannah and Rhonda finalized their thoughts into a plan that answered the following questions:

1. What is the main strategy for volunteer recruitment? A general call for people? A request for specific skills?
2. How should Hannah and Rhonda approach the community groups?
3. What should be the timeframe for the recruitment efforts?

Other questions to consider:

1. What is the benefit of a museum's volunteer corps, staff, and/or board reflecting its community demographics?
2. Is the Copperfield overreacting to the news stories?
3. What are the key objectives for a museum's volunteer recruitment plan?

CASE 3: BERLIN HISTORICAL SOCIETY

When attendance and donation projections for a new wing fail to meet their goals, the Berlin Historical Society must reduce expenses. Director Tonya Dunston asks each department to create a staff plan that lists employees to be laid off. Concerned that Tonya is acting to benefit her own career prospects, the department heads decide to craft an alternative cost-cutting plan and consider notifying the media.

Berlin Historical Society Background

Though it was only fifty years old, the Berlin Historical Society enjoyed a national reputation and typically a robust revenue stream. Crescent City had decided to create a historical society to preserve and memorialize the scientific discoveries at the nearby national laboratory. The lab focused on applied engineering, but hadn't worked on the more exciting space or atomic projects. After county funds were allocated for the new historical society, residents argued that the historical society should encompass all of Berlin County's history, including indigenous peoples and suffragettes, who had launched the first statewide auto campaign from Crescent City. Begrudgingly, the society's founders agreed that the society's mission should be to preserve and interpret the history of the residents of Berlin County, not just the history of the national lab.

The tensions and disagreements of those founding days continued. Board seats were held by family and friends of the original board. Exhibitions about the suffragettes and indigenous peoples were marginalized. The board hired directors after a national search. The Berlin's five million dollar budget, award-winning exhibitions, and popular programs made its directorship a popular stepping stone to larger institutions. The department heads were a mix of local citizens and out-of-town recruits. The remaining staff and volunteers were local residents. Since the directors only stayed for a few years, the department heads, who tended to stay for many years, learned to accommodate the career goals of the incumbent director with the visitors' expectations.

The New Wing

The board hired Tonya Dunston to shepherd the construction of a new wing. A prominent family donated 25 percent of the construction cost and a collection of equipment from the national laboratory. Tonya and the board hired a consulting firm to project attendance for the new wing. The firm concluded that attendance would increase by 50 percent. The resulting revenue increase would support the maintenance costs of the new wing and the hiring of additional staff.

Shelley Hughes, the sales director, pointed out that many people had similar equipment sitting in their garages. The new collection at the historical society represented the breadth of the lab's work, but lacked the unique or rare artifact that would spur visitation. Tonya and the board were convinced that the curatorial staff's prowess at designing compelling exhibitions would attract visitors.

The first signs of trouble appeared during the fundraising. Previous big money donors told James Behar, the development director, that they would not donate to the new wing. They felt that the new wing was more about flattering a certain family than fulfilling the society's mission. Some mid-level donors were upset that the women's suffrage document digitization project was postponed to focus staff resources on the new wing and its collection. Consequently, the fundraising campaign only reached 80 percent of its goal. The board then approved a special withdrawal from the endowment to mitigate the shortfall. City newspapers editorialized against that maneuver.

The Opening

The concerns about the fundraising shortfall and the ambitious attendance projections did not dampen enthusiasm for the opening of the new wing. Local dignitaries attended. The reviews of the architecture and the new exhibits were uniformly positive. The visitor comment cards were enthusiastic. Attendance increased by 5 percent in the first month. After a few months, attendance returned to its normal levels. The increased expenses were not offset by additional revenue, so the Berlin was faced with a significant deficit. The board did not understand why the actual attendance diverged from the projection.

Tonya understood that the new wing was a risk. She planned to move onto a new job within a year of the opening. She had thought that the new wing was a calculated risk and assumed that the fundraising would more than cover the construction costs. She had estimated that attendance would only increase by 10 or 15 percent. Her plan was to task the development department with identifying and writing additional grants to support the suffrage document digitization and other projects. The revenue goals for the store and facility rentals would also increase.

When the fundraising failed to reach goal, Tonya began suggesting to the board that salary freezes or staff cuts might be necessary as a short-term measure to balance the budget. Of course, the recession had an adverse effect on discretionary spending. When the economy recovered, the attendance projection would prove accurate. More importantly, Tonya's leadership and problem-solving skills would be evident to her next employer.

Tonya and the board met four months after the wing opening and agreed that staff reductions were the most effective solution to the revenue shortfall. They decided that four of the thirty-three full-time staff positions should be eliminated. In the interest of fairness, each department head would be required to submit a staff plan to justify head count and to suggest candidates for layoffs.

The Staff Meeting

At the next staff meeting, Tonya announced the board's decision.

"These are incredibly difficult decisions," said Tonya. "I felt it was important for everyone to be involved—in the interest of fairness. The board agreed."

"I'm a little confused about the numbers," said Mary Rydell, the program and education director. "We have five departments: Marketing, Sales, Programs and Education, Development and Membership, and Curatorial. So is each department supposed to nominate one person? Then who decides which four will be laid off? Or if our staff plan shows that two or three people might be considered for layoffs, will more than four people be laid off?"

"What other costs will be reduced?" asked Shelley Hughes, the sales director. "I think we should suspend reimbursements for professional association memberships, conference expenses, and professional development. We could also freeze staff salaries. Have we thought about ways to increase revenue? I have been pushing for an increase in admission for several years, especially with the new wing. An additional dollar per fee category would help tremendously. We also should charge a premium for rentals in the new wing. Layoffs should be a last resort, not a first resort."

"Well the board looked at many options," replied Tonya. "Staff reductions have the most immediate impact on finances. Increasing admission and facility rentals fees are options, but that revenue generation will take longer. Unfortunately, we don't have the luxury of time to balance this year's budget. I'll expect your staff plans on my desk by the end of the week."

The meeting then proceeded through the rest of the agenda. The department heads decided to lunch together off-site the following day.

The Staff Lunch

"I can't believe you suggested cutting professional memberships and development," said Linda Jones, the marketing director.

"Only Tonya and the board receive those benefits. They're responsible for this mess and should bear some of the burden," said Shelley.

"Since my department failed to meet the fundraising goal," said James, "we should bear the brunt of the layoffs."

"You can't guarantee that each campaign will meet goal. I couldn't guarantee a 50 percent increase in attendance," said Shelley. "Those numbers were unrealistic."

"I was surprised that the board didn't push to combine marketing and development or marketing and sales," said Linda. "Other museums do that. The board keeps reducing my budget. I thought for sure Tonya was going to announce the elimination of my department at the staff meeting."

"She does enjoy public humiliation," observed Mary. "She has the board wrapped around her finger."

"Because she sends them gift baskets of new store items that come out of my budget and pays for their memberships in museum and board associations. Cut that fat first," said Shelley.

"She needs a balanced budget, so she can say that she prevented a fiscal disaster during her next job interview," said Lindsay Canfield, the curatorial director.

"Which solves her problem, but not ours," said Mary. "We're going to be here after she's left. How can we salvage the situation?"

"I have three people who would be happy to move to part-time status," said Shelley. "It eliminates part of a salary and all the benefits."

"I could make do with one curatorial assistant," said Lindsay.

"No," replied Shelley and James in unison.

"You and Mary have small departments that are already overworked," said James. "I am fortunate to have six staff members. Roy is close to retirement and receives benefits through his wife's job. He has already approached me about the situation. He knows layoffs will happen and offered himself as a candidate."

"Everyone on the marketing team is looking for new jobs. Two people have already had second interviews, so we may lose them soon," said Linda.

"Our tally is three for layoff and three for part-time," said Shelley. "Is that enough?"

"By the end of the week, I will find out about our grant applications," said Mary. "If we receive all three, then all of our education programs and staff will be covered."

"Fingers crossed," said Lindsay. "James, how close are we to securing the donation for the suffragette digitization project?"

"Mrs. Marigold is close to writing a check. I think she wants one more lunch to complain about the new wing. Then she should be ready to sign."

"Do you think she would sign the check faster if she knew about the staff cuts?" asked Linda.

"That's tricky. She could view it as one more sign of incompetence and stop supporting the society all together. Sharing internal issues with donors isn't a good idea."

"Even I would draw that line," laughed Shelley.

"What if we told everyone?" asked Linda.

Silence descended. Newspaper editorials and public opinion were against the new wing, primarily due to the financial issues. Disclosing impending staff cuts could have significant unforeseen consequences.

"Publicly humiliating Tonya could cost all of us our jobs," said Mary. "The media regularly covers us. Tonya will slip the layoff news into one of her press releases. Then we will see what happens."

"After people have lost their jobs," argued Linda.

"Our goal should be carrying out the society's mission to the best of our abilities, regardless of our personal feelings," said Lindsay.

"How can the society focus on its mission if the director prioritizes her career over the museum?" asked Linda.

"We don't know how many people will be laid off. Tonya and the board may be happy with our suggestions, which solve the problem with buy-in. A public fight pitting board and director against the museum staff could cost more jobs, memberships, and gifts. Let's proceed cautiously," said James.

"I agree," said Shelley. "We have a fair compromise. Mary and I can include additional recommendations for increasing revenue. We'll know about the educational grants in a day or two. Let's not create a problem that we truly can't solve. Eventually the press will find out. We'll see how much public support we actually have."

Everyone agreed to focus on their individual staff plans and wait for reactions from Tonya and the board before considering a press leak. The others were concerned that Linda still might notify the press. As they worked on their staff plans, they contemplated the following questions:

1. Although the staff was instructed to focus on reduction recommendations, how can revenue increase recommendations be incorporated?
2. What balance should be struck between the personal circumstances of staff members and the needs of the institution?
3. How can departments work together to fulfill the institution's mission?

Other questions to consider:

1. How should the staff balance personal career goals with institutional goals?
2. Is Tonya really incorporating the staff into the decision-making process?
3. Is it ethical for museum personnel (director or staff) to notify the media about internal disputes? Why or why not?

EPILOGUE

Interpersonal relationships and interpretations of goals are the core issues for all three case studies. The James Benjamin House Museum is evolving and expanding, but one volunteer is potentially hindering future success. The Copperfield Botanical Garden is confronting perceptions of elitism; its board and staff are considering strategies to expand their recruitment pools. They can't control the outcomes of their efforts. Budget pressures at the Berlin County Historical Society are exposing long-standing disagreements among the board, museum director, museum staff, and donors.

Learning to work with different personality types is a challenge in every environment. The working relationships and personal connections among museum staff directly impact the institution's ability to fulfill its mission. When staff members are willing to work together, despite their differences, positive outcomes can be reached. If not, changes in personnel will be the only solution.

Chapter 4

Collection Management

INTRODUCTION

Collection management is the heart of the public trust with museums. As stewards of the collection, museum personnel must balance research needs, public visitation, and conservation needs to preserve and share the objects. Though the tools and techniques used to achieve that balance may change over time, institutions can still develop clear collection management policies to guide staff and record institutional memory.

This chapter features three case studies exploring:

- collection management policies;
- scholarly versus marketing points of view;
- deaccessioning; and
- public stewardship.

Even with the best of intentions, museum staff may interpret museum codes of ethics or collection management policies differently. Having these policies and affirming ethical codes provide the parameters for decisions about the collection. As you develop solutions to the questions asked at the end of each case study, consider how your interpretations of museum association ethical codes and your internal collection management policies complement one another or leave gaps. These case studies may also raise additional ethical questions that the characters don't recognize, but you may contemplate those questions when formulating your responses.

CASE 1: BYRD ART MUSEUM

The Byrd Art Museum houses an eclectic collection of European paintings and artifacts purchased by local businessman Fred Byrd after World War I. Since the collection's provenance and attributions are tenuous, the Byrd's mission focuses on educating people about such issues. New scholarship implies that one of the Byrd's paintings is an actual Rembrandt. Margot Nicoletti, the curator, is proceeding cautiously, while Lynne Jefferson, the marketing and development director, wants to publicize the Byrd's "new" Rembrandt.

Museum Background

Founded in 1925, the Byrd Art Museum presented the collection of Fred Byrd. Inspired by art seen during his World War I service, Fred returned to Europe after the war and acquired paintings, sculpture, and a few suits of armor from ruined aristocrats. He believed that since Americans had earned a place on the world stage during the war, they needed to learn more about Europe and its culture. Fred's dream was to acquire, disassemble, ship, and reassemble a castle in his hometown of Augusta, but his father refused to release enough money from Fred's trust fund to enable the purchase of a castle.

Making due with local limestone and marble, Fred commissioned a grand Gilded Age style manor and installed his collection. As the only cultural institution in a hundred mile radius, the Byrd enjoyed an annual attendance between twenty-five thousand and thirty thousand people. Fred's quirky personality and collecting philosophy allowed the museum staff to explore issues like the serviceman's experience in World War I, the United States' entry into world affairs after the war, American collectors in Europe, artists' workshops, and copies/forgeries—especially after most of the paintings were revealed to be copies or attributed to artists' workshops.

The Byrd Family Endowment, admission fees, and donations generated the museum's two hundred fifty thousand dollar annual budget. Special projects, including the conservation of artifacts and exhibitions, were funded by grants or targeted fundraising campaigns. The museum's staff of four full-time employees, six part-time employees, and twenty volunteers were primarily local citizens and tended to remain at the Byrd for their entire careers.

The "New" Rembrandt

"It's real!" exclaimed Lynne Jefferson, the director of marketing and development. "Scholars and visitors from around the world will come to see it!"

"It's been real and unreal for eighty years," said Corinne Mead, the museum director. "The key Rembrandt scholars have seen it and are divided. When my dad was curator in the 1970s, the same thing happened. That's why we have our Mystery Painting program."

"But this attribution is really strong. We can use it to strengthen grant applications and appeal to funders."

"Oh, Lynne, we aren't a million dollar campaign museum. Our biggest donor can only afford to give us ten thousand dollars. If the painting is a real Rembrandt, we couldn't afford the insurance or security. That's why we have the deal with the Cedar Junction Art Museum for loans of the really valuable artifacts."

"We don't even try. The building is in good shape and pretty secure. We have about a dozen paintings now that are real. People come from all over the world to ski here. They would also come here to see real art."

"They already come to see the fake art."

"They come to laugh and put slugs in the collection boxes. We could get real money if we are a real art museum."

"Margot has a better sense of the art world; talk to her. Then you two can create a plan for handling the Rembrandt."

The Byrd's Reputation

Early in her career, Margot Nicoletti, the Byrd's curator, recognized the limitations of the Byrd's collection and its lowbrow reputation. Since her husband was the vice president at the local bank, Margot knew she would remain in Augusta and decided to embrace the eccentricities of the Byrd's collection. Her research into Rembrandt's apprentices won awards. She was widely regarded as a leading scholar of post–World War I era American art collectors. In her office she displayed a purse that looked like a pig's ear to remind herself and the rest of the staff that silk purses and sow's ears can be the same thing, but are still different.

Margot became the head curator ten years ago, promoted after Corinne's father retired. She was well aware of the fluctuating attributions of the Rembrandt and enjoyed reading each new evaluation. Privately, Margot believed it was a Rembrandt. Publicly, she remained neutral because the evidence was not definitive.

She knew Lynne would be excited about the new attribution. Lynne had joined the Byrd when Margot was promoted to head curator. The reputation of the collection thwarted Lynne's grant applications and appeals to foundations. The Cedar Junction deal was a problem for both Lynne and Margot.

When a painting was definitively attributed to a significant artist, it was sent on long-term loan to the Cedar Junction Art Museum, a large institution with state-of-the-art security and conservation capabilities. Cedar Junction paid an annual loan fee to the Byrd and assumed the conservation, insurance, and security obligations for the item. Corinne's father had negotiated the deal when a Pissarro was authenticated. As long as an attribution was not definitive, the object remained at the Byrd. Margot wanted the Rembrandt to remain. When Lynne entered Margot's office, Margot realized that she might be forced to publicly state her private opinions.

Lynne and Margot Meet

Lynne explained her grand plan to reclaim the Cedar Junction loans. The agreement did allow the Byrd to rescind the loans with six months' notice. No one thought that the Byrd would ever be in a financial position to afford to reclaim the objects, but the Byrd had to retain ownership per the terms of Byrd Family Endowment. Lynne thought the Rembrandt could be the cornerstone of a new section of real paintings. The new authentication would generate scholarly and funder interest that would benefit the entire collection.

"This could be our only chance to establish a serious section of the museum," said Lynne. "The crazy Mr. Byrd story is fun, but hurts our reputation."

"The story is really how Mr. Byrd's lack of knowledge and immense enthusiasm led to some unfortunate acquisitions, like other collectors of his era," replied Margot.

"Margot."

"Our mission is to help people appreciate art and advance their art education."

"Because our collection consists mainly of fakes and knock-offs. Yes, we're doing the best we can in our circumstances. Now we have a chance to be taken seriously. Weren't you excited when you heard the Rembrandt news?

"The new scholarship is very exciting. I was impressed with the level of detail and analysis of the evidence. I e-mailed the author my congratulations."

"You know him?"

"A little bit. Obviously, he came here to see the painting. We have appeared on panels together."

"Could he come here and discuss our painting?"

"His authentication of our painting has the weakest evidence. We would need to present both sides."

"That would be great! We would get international coverage. We could present a symposium of Rembrandt scholars. This could be huge."

"Well, we don't have the money to host a symposium. If we decide the painting is a Rembrandt, the board will send it to Cedar Junction," said Margot.

Lynne replied, "The agreement doesn't technically require us to automatically send an object to Cedar Junction after an authentication. Our board has to vote to submit the loan request to Cedar Junction; their board has to vote to approve the request. If our board does vote for a loan request, Cedar Junction has no power."

"Then we incur the insurance, conservation, and security costs."

"I've already contacted some Rembrandt appreciators. Three of them can't afford a big city museum wing or donation, but could afford to underwrite us. The building is solid limestone, brick, and marble. Our insurance guys think that a few more guards, cameras, and alarms will meet their requirements. Then we can easily reclaim the Pissarro and other objects. Come on, Margot. You know what this would mean to Augusta."

"Do you have a written agreement for the donations?"

"The board has to vote to agree with the authentication first."

"What did Corinne say?"

"She said you and I should create a plan, accounting for your interpretation of the art world's reaction. Will the authentication be considered credible?"

Margot paused, "If other scholars agree with the attribution, the authentication will probably be considered credible."

"You don't seem enthused. Do you disagree with the attribution? Do you want the painting to go to Cedar Junction?"

"I always want the objects to be cared for and to be accessible to visitors and scholars. If we ourselves can't provide that environment and have access to such an environment, we should act in the best interest of the object."

"What about the attribution?"

"It is the strongest scholarship I have seen."

"So you agree it's a Rembrandt."

"I can't say with a 100 percent certainty."

"Margot!"

"I can't! There's no definitive answer, which is why I support the painting remaining here with a tentative authentication."

"What does that mean?"

"We can say it came from Rembrandt's studio and has been attributed to Rembrandt himself by some scholars."

"What about the return of the other objects?"

"Under current circumstances, I can't guarantee optimal conservation or insurance conditions."

Lynne thought for a few minutes and said, "So sounds like you would be open to a Rembrandt symposium to debate the attribution."

"If you can obtain the funding, I am happy to invite the scholars and organize the program."

"Then we can reclaim the Cedar Junction objects after the symposium."

"The symposium will provide Corinne and the board with a sense of the response of the art community and help guide future decisions about the Rembrandt and other objects."

"You must be an excellent poker player, Margot. I bet you win every time."

"No. I do mitigate my losses."

Lynne and Margot began to draft a symposium proposal that must answer the following questions:

1. What is the purpose of the symposium?
2. How will the scholarly debate inform the pragmatic decisions about the painting?
3. How does the Byrd's mission impact the "need" for the Byrd to have authentic art objects?

Other questions to consider:

1. Should Margot publicly declare her opinion about the Rembrandt? Why or why not?
2. How did the Cedar Junction agreement impact the Byrd?
3. What are the ethical issues raised by the Cedar Junction agreement?

CASE 2: LLOYD NATURAL HISTORY MUSEUM

The Lloyd Natural History Museum features an array of taxidermy animals and geological samples. In the 1950s, a donor gave the museum three Frederick Remington paintings and five Ansel Adams prints to "set the scene" in the galleries. The insurance and conservation costs are now overwhelming the museum. Board President John Collins wants to sell some or all of the paintings and prints. Museum Director Adam Perry and Curatorial Director Sidney Doyle are concerned about the ethical and reputation issues created by deaccessioning.

Museum Background

Named after its town, the Lloyd Natural History Museum was founded in 1938. A Civilian Conservation Corps (CCC) project yielded rock specimens, which were combined with samples from the local taxidermy shop. As a former frontier town, Lloyd wanted to memorialize that landscape. Dioramas that recreated the plains seemed like the perfect solution. Volunteers staffed the small building and taught local history to schoolchildren. When local businessman Spencer

Cooper died in 1951, he left his art collection, consisting of the Remingtons and Adamses, to be displayed to evoke the old landscapes. In the 1990s, three of the Adams prints and two of the Remington paintings were put in storage due to concerns about their fragility. Hung in direct sunlight, fading had occurred. The museum could not afford the restoration costs.

The Lloyd was popular within its eponymous town of thirty thousand and had an annual visitation of seven thousand. The staff was all part-time, and many had visited the Lloyd as schoolchildren. Those visits inspired them to work at the Lloyd to teach other schoolchildren about nature—the cornerstone of the Lloyd's mission. The museum's annual haunted house, hunting season parties, and nature walks were popular. Admission and program fees, gift shop sales, and facility rental revenues barely covered the thirty thousand dollar annual budget.

Budget discussions were always tense. Adam Perry, the museum director, was dreading the upcoming review with John Collins, the board president. The FBI had notified Adam about a series of robberies of Frederick Remington paintings from small museums and private collections. The FBI theorized that one collector had hired a group of art thieves to steal Remington paintings. The subject matter and valuations varied, so the FBI assumed that all Remingtons were potential targets. The board had asked Adam to get insurance quotes for both the Remingtons and the Adamses.

The Quote Review

Adam and John typically met two weeks before the board's annual budget meeting to review the proposed budget and any other financial matters. This year, they scheduled the meeting four weeks prior, assuming that the insurance situation would be complicated. Cost was the only real issue. Adam discovered that insuring just one of the Remingtons or Adamses would cost more than thirty thousand dollars. He knew that John would be displeased.

Adam presented John with a comparison of all the insurance quotes and waited for John's reaction.

"Are you kidding me?" asked John. "These numbers are ridiculous. Did you get the non-profit price?"

"Yes," replied Adam. "Remington and Adams are popular. With the current string of Remington thefts, the insurance companies have raised the premiums."

"Gouging! They're gouging for some paintings of horses and pictures of trees!"

". . . from a renowned artist and a very important photographer."

"I don't care how important they are in the art world. This isn't an art museum. These things just hang on the walls. Not all of them even hang on the walls. These things have been a financial nightmare for twenty years."

"We have been applying for grants to clean and restore all of them. Eventually, we will win one."

"Really? A small natural history museum in the middle of a prairie is going to get an art grant from East Coasters?"

"The National Czech and Slovak Museum and Library got grants. They're in Cedar Rapids."

"Their entire building flooded! Everything had to be rebuilt and cleaned. That's more exciting than a few paintings and photos. We should just get rid of them."

"They are accessioned into the collection. We can't just get rid of them."

"Why not?"

"A museum holds its collection for the public good. People give to the museum with the understanding that the museum will preserve and share those objects with the public. Ethically, you are only allowed to deaccession and sell pieces from the collection if you are going to use that money for other acquisitions."

"Another East Coast rule."

"It's a museum professional rule. Selling pieces from the collection is the lazy way to earn money if the board and staff fail to properly budget or fundraise. The value of the collection is educational not financial."

"So we can sell the stuff if we use the money to buy a stuffed elk."

"Um . . . yes," said Adam, who then prepared for another outburst from John. Instead, John sat quietly for a few minutes, thinking before he spoke again.

"So," began John, "museum professionals would rather a museum close and dump its collection than sell a few things to keep the doors open."

"I don't want to say that," said Adam.

"Here's the deal. We can't afford the insurance for this stuff. The bank is willing to keep it all locked up in the vault without charging a storage fee, but that means I owe my brother-in-law a favor. I don't like owing him favors. We'd also have to draft some legal agreements about the storage—more money down the drain. When the board meets, I am going to recommend selling the whole lot. If we don't, we'll bankrupt the museum; if not now, then at some point in the future. You and the museum staff have four weeks to figure out another plan that isn't going to cost us money or favors. Forget the grants. I want cash in hand."

Adam agreed to John's ultimatum. In his heart, he doubted that the staff could create a plan that fit John's parameters. If they could reduce some of the financial costs, they might be able to persuade the other board members to save the Remingtons and Adamses.

The Staff Meets

Later that afternoon, Adam met with Ralph Doyle, the museum curator, and Molly Engels, the marketing and communications coordinator.

"That's what I like about John," laughed Molly. "He doesn't sugarcoat it. He does represent the opinions of most of the board, unfortunately."

"The big problem is that none of us have a professional museum education," said Adam. "I've read a lot about deaccessioning, but I wasn't comfortable answering John's questions about it."

"Actually the big problem is that the Remingtons and Adamses are the highlights of the collection, though they were never meant to be so," said Ralph. "Honestly, I can't say that we are good stewards for those pieces. The sun fading on the Remingtons is an embarrassment. For their own protection, we should work out some type of agreement with another museum; maybe a loan."

"We tried five years ago. The other museums balked at the restoration costs. The damage is so bad. A private collector offered to buy all three, but we didn't pursue the offer," said Adam.

"Did John know about the offer?" asked Molly.

"No, Len was the board president and opposed any collection sales. I don't think he even told the rest of the board," said Adam.

"Do you think that collector or another collector would be willing to donate the restoration or insurance funds?" asked Molly.

"They want to own the paintings. They might donate to a big city museum and get their name on a wing. They aren't interested in sponsoring the Hall of Foxes, which by the way has a Remington hanging on the wall," said Adam.

"My kid's friend has one of those Indiegogo campaigns to raise money for his zombie movie," said Ralph. "We could do a Remington restoration campaign. The publicity would be helpful. If we are successful, that might help our grant chances."

"We are also letting the thieves know about our Remingtons," said Molly.

"They already know," said Adam. "Last week, they stole the two Remingtons stored in the basement of the Chester Allen House. If they know about those paintings, they know about ours."

"What about the Adams prints?" asked Molly. "They're prints, so they aren't really unique. Is it less bad to deaccession and sell them?"

"That's a slippery slope," said Ralph. "You are setting the precedent of selling your collection. The specifics don't matter. We're breaking the public's trust and the donor's trust."

"So there's no compromise—even in exigent circumstances," said Molly. "We have to keep the paintings and photos. We'll have to forgo the insurance and restoration."

"The other thefts have made the board nervous," said Adam. "I think they are looking for a way to get rid of the paintings and the photos for sure to avoid a similar situation in the future. No one knows who we are, so we might be able to deaccession and sell without notice. We aren't accredited, so we won't lose that. After the Delaware Art Museum and Babson situations, the museum and art media are looking for these types of stories. I don't want us to start a national reputation as a bad museum. The *New York Times* called about the Remington thefts. I've read the AAM, AASLH, and AAMD guidelines and still don't know what to do. I don't want to post on message boards and get yelled at. I want to do the best thing for the museum, but I don't know what that is."

"We all feel like that," said Ralph. "We can't afford to keep them. We can't afford to maintain them. We ethically can't sell them . . . unless we recategorize them."

"What do you mean?" asked Adam.

"Well, our mission is to educate the children of Lloyd about nature and our local past. Technically, the Remingtons and Adamses fall outside the mission. The scenes aren't local. Our point of view has always been the actual objects, like the taxidermy specimens trump artistic representations. We refused that other donation of paintings in the 1970s."

"John will love it," said Molly. "We'll all hate ourselves, but I can't think of another way."

"I already hate myself for saying it. I hate myself more when I see the damaged paintings and know I can't help them. What do you think, Adam?" asked Ralph.

"Private collectors will be the only people willing to buy them in this condition, so the public won't have access to them," said Adam. "Not that anyone is making a special trip to the Lloyd. We can justify it anyway we want, but we're doing something wrong. I'm not blaming you, Ralph. It kills all of us to see those damaged paintings. I guess we don't have any other choice."

Adam, Ralph, and Molly then wrote their recommendation to the board, which answered the following questions:

1. Is Ralph's solution ethical? Why or why not?
2. What options should the board consider for the Frederick Remington paintings and Ansel Adams prints?
3. What are the consequences of each option to the paintings and prints?

Other questions to consider:

1. How does a museum balance ethical and pragmatic concerns?

2. What is the relationship between the museum's mission and potential deaccessioning issues?
3. Is deaccessioning ethical under any circumstances? Why or why not?

CASE 3: CHANDLERVILLE HISTORICAL SOCIETY

The Chandlerville Historical Society suffers the sudden loss of longtime curator Barbara Castle, who was well-respected and loved by the community. In preparation for an upcoming exhibit and as a matter of protocol, new curator Meg Payton conducts an inventory and discovers that an important artifact is missing. As events unfold, Meg and Alexis Sheridan, the director, reconsider their collection management policies and procedures.

Museum Background

The Chandlerville Historical Society evolved from the Chandlerville Ladies Society in the 1940s. The original purpose was to bring cultural or scholarly lectures to Chandlerville. As the organization changed, the Historical Society's mission also included providing cultural and scholarly experiences for the Chandlerville community, as well as preserving and sharing local history.

The townspeople supported the historical society. In a town of seventy thousand, the society enjoyed annual attendance of thirty-five thousand. Donations, admission and program fees, gift shop sales, and facility rental revenues comfortably met or surpassed the three hundred thousand dollar annual budget.

Barbara Castle, the longtime curator, began her career as assistant registrar at a major metropolitan art museum. She moved to Chandlerville for the opportunity to be a curator and had been the head curator for fifteen years. Her sudden death shocked and saddened the staff and community. Meg Payton, the assistant curator, was promoted to head curator.

Per the Chandlerville collection management procedural manual, any change in the head curator position triggered an automatic inventory. Everyone assumed that the results would be the same as the regularly scheduled spring inventory.

The Inventory Results

Meg entered Alexis Sheridan's office. Alexis had been the director for five years and had been recruited from another historical society.

"So is everything okay?" asked Alexis. "Are we still at 5 percent missing?"

"Overall, yes," said Meg. "We do have a problem. The Chandler Coin Collection is missing."

"It's not in the vault?"

"Nope, I took everything out. I opened every single box. I checked all the storage areas and tore apart Barbara's desk."

"What about Past Perfect? Are there any notes?"

"There's nothing. She had a notebook about the upcoming exhibit about collections. The coins are the key object in that exhibit, so I was surprised that there weren't any comments. The insurance appraisal already happened, and they came back from conservation last month. I don't know where they could be."

Alexis thought for a few moments and then said, "We will proceed under the assumption that the coins are here in the building. Barbara may have been working with them and didn't return them to the vault, as per protocol. We all make mistakes. Ask Ann to recheck all the storage spaces and the vault. We'll reconnect in the afternoon."

Ann was the academic and public program coordinator. She and Barbara had been working on the exhibition. Alexis hoped that Ann knew the coins whereabouts. Barbara had been an excellent curator, but was a poor communicator. She had routinely excluded Meg from meetings and did not share her thoughts and actions with others. She did what she thought was best. She resisted Alexis' insistence on keeping Past Perfect up-to-date and logging items that were out for conservation. She was upset when Meg, who was hired a year after Alexis, suggested assigning each storage area a unique ID. Barbara liked being the go-to person for the collection, which now had serious repercussions.

Alexis wasn't surprised that Barbara neglected to leave a note about the coins and decided to call Barbara's husband. Unfortunately, Barbara hadn't mentioned the coins to him. Alexis knew she would have to notify the board if the coins weren't found by the end of the day.

The Coin Search

Meg watched as Ann carefully removed every item from the vault, opened each box and envelope, and double-checked the inventory.

"Don't worry," said Ann. "I'm sure the coins are here somewhere. You know Barbara. She thought she was indispensable and proved it by not updating records. You won't be blamed."

"But I'm the curator. I'm responsible for the collection. I was here before. How can the board not blame me? I should have kept an eye on the coins. They're too important."

"Stop. You couldn't have watched the coins 24/7. Both Alexis and the board have been happy with you. Barbara gave you glowing performance reviews. This just proves Alexis's point about the importance of communications and record keeping. Maybe we'll get the Institute of Museum and Library Services (IMLS) grant to RFID the collection (i.e., use radio-frequency identification)."

Ann repeated her careful examination of the storages areas to no avail. She then proceeded to Barbara's desk.

"So the coins have already been to conservation?" asked Ann.

"Yes," said Meg.

"The appraisers came here?"

"Yes, they review objects on site. They check the security at the same time."

After Ann read all of Barbara's notes and phone messages, she said, "The last comment about the coins relates to Cummings Company. Aren't they the cabinet fabricators?"

"Yes," said Meg. "They came here to measure and photograph the coins. They're bringing a couple of cases next week, so we can see how they look in the space."

"They wouldn't have the coins?"

"They shouldn't have the coins. Al Cummings always insists that he can't build the case unless he has the object on site for inspiration. Private collectors let him do that. His museum clients don't. He whines and then builds the cases."

"He and Barbara are friends. Is it possible that she bent the rules for him?"

"She did let the photographer remove those two busts. I guess anything is possible."

Ann called Cummings and discovered that he did have the coins.

"No," said Ann. "Meg is leaving here immediately to pick up the coins. You will have them ready for her. You will not have one of your employees deliver them. Meg is insured and bonded by the museum. You and your staff are not. Just have the coins ready."

Ann hung up the phone and sent Meg to pick up the coins. She went to Alexis's office and explained the situation.

Ann and Alexis Debrief

"I can't believe Barbara did that," said Alexis.

"She probably thought she could pick up the coins before coming to work on Monday and trusted that Al would keep them safe since he always has valuable items on premises," said Ann. "Meg is blaming herself. She didn't know."

"Meg would have told us if she knew what Barbara was planning," said Alexis. "Barbara made a bad decision. She knew our insurance wouldn't cover any off-site incidents. She let her friendship with Al color her judgment. The question now is how do we prevent a similar incident?"

"We already have at least two people completing the annual inventory and require a sign off on the policy and procedures manuals. We require updates to Past Perfect and the custody log. It's human nature to make mistakes or cut corners. I don't think we can do anything else."

"When Meg returns, we need to discuss the situation and ensure it doesn't happen again. I also have to explain what happened to the board," said Alexis.

As Alexis and Ann awaited Meg's return, they considered the following questions in preparation for the board discussion:

1. What protocols could be instituted to prevent a similar situation?
2. Should the society continue to use Cummings? Why or why not?
3. Since Alexis knew Barbara did not always follow the correct procedures, should Barbara have been warned and possibly terminated for disobeying procedures in prior months?

Other questions to consider:

1. How should employees be disciplined for violating policies?
2. How can technologies like RFID resolved staff member attitude and/or missing item problems?
3. What channels should be available for junior employees to share concerns about senior employees?

EPILOGUE

Ethics and decision-making skills are the core of all three case studies. The Byrd Art Museum is grappling with the oxymoronic problem of having an authentic Rembrandt. The Lloyd Natural History Museum has artistically significant holdings that are deteriorating and theoretically unrelated to the museum's mission; its board president sees deaccessioning and selling the artifacts as the obvious answer. The Chandlerville Historical Society was confronted with a tragic staff loss that unwittingly exposed a poor collection management decision.

The pragmatic realities of past decisions, revenue limitations, and object conditions might seem more important than theoretical codes of ethics. The point of these codes is to provide a series of principals to guide decisions. By learning those principals, you can consider all of your options and possibilities before being confronted with difficult choices and try to avoid the circumstances described in these cases.

Chapter 5

Exhibition Planning

INTRODUCTION

Exhibition planning is the first step in creating the most visible intersection of a museum's collections and mission: the exhibition. Permanent or temporary, traveling or stationary, exhibitions are the key communications platform between the museum staff and the public. The museum staff creates exhibitions to educate, inspire, or provoke the public, who in turn respond through attendance, commentary, or the lack thereof. Exhibitions may also chart the path for programs and education activities. The cost of exhibitions can be a significant percentage of a museum's budget.

This chapter features three case studies exploring:

• definitions of an exhibition's success or failure;
• guest feedback and reactions;
• the use of traveling exhibitions or reconstructions; and
• the board's role in the exhibition planning process.

Exhibition planning can be a stressful and fulfilling activity. It is also a vital public expression of the institution's mission and scholarship. As you develop solutions to the questions asked at the end of each case study, consider how your institution plans exhibitions and the impact of mission and budget on those plans.

CASE 1: LAMPE NATURE MUSEUM

The Lampe Nature Museum maintains a strict exhibition schedule: four exhibits per year—one per season. The exhibitions use objects from the collection and reflect the current season. The exhibition openings also kick-off membership drives and fundraising campaigns. Recently, the Lampe's exhibitions have been perceived as unsuccessful. Donors are unenthused, and attendance has dipped. Reviews in the local media have been lukewarm. Curator Miriam Yang is under pressure to invigorate the exhibitions or face dismissal.

Museum Background

Sheila Lampe was the last member of a formerly prominent family in the city of Oakley. She lived as a recluse in the old family home, which was surrounded by twenty acres of land. When Sheila died in 1925, she left her house, land, and small fortune to the city to be preserved as a nature museum. When officials entered the home, they found it in good condition. Sheila had extensive collections of flora, fauna, and taxidermy animals, which were all extensively researched and catalogued. They also found Sheila's pet cobra, which was promptly sent to the zoo. No one knew how Sheila had obtained her specimens and pet, but the first museum staff decided that those twin pillars of serious scholarship and surprise would provide the foundation for the museum's endeavors.

Over the ensuing decades, those pillars evolved into a mission of facilitating the exploration of nature, ecology, and conservation and surprising guests with unexpected experiences. Due to the financial prudence of the boards, Sheila's small fortune grew into a ten million dollar endowment that contributed to a three million dollar annual budget. That budget enabled the museum staff to develop award-winning and innovative exhibitions and programs for the hundred thousand visitors each year. The pressure of maintaining that level of excellence also created staff burnout. The typical head curator or program director had a three- to five-year tenure at the Lampe. When the board became dissatisfied with the head curator or program director, they communicated that dissatisfaction to the museum director, who then dismissed the staff member. Alums of the Lampe were prized by other museums, so they were usually able to find new jobs relatively quickly. The experience was still unpleasant.

Miriam Yang had been the head curator for three years. Her experience as an assistant curator at several large natural history museums and as a painter had intrigued the board. Miriam's exhibit design renderings were displayed with the exhibitions to show guests how the ideas became reality.

Exhibition Reception

Though the staff and board had been enthusiastic about Miriam's previous two exhibits, *The Folklore of Ladybugs* and *The Mighty Oak*, the donors and guests were not. Exhibition attendance and fundraising totals dipped. When queried, neither the donors nor the guests could articulate their reasons for disappointment. They just said that past exhibitions were better.

Miriam recognized that she was in the three- to five-year dismissal time-frame. She understood that reality when she accepted the job. The Lampe was her first opportunity as a head curator and would support her creativity. Lampe curators and program directors were given creative freedom and generous budgets and expected to maintain the institution's high standards. No one wants to be fired. Miriam had grown close to the rest of the staff. As she prepared for her weekly meeting with the assistant curator, Christine Jarrett, Miriam wondered what her fate would be.

"Knock, knock," said Christine.

"Come in," said Miriam. "Do you have the guest survey summary?"

"Yes. The responses are pretty vague. I can't figure out what we are doing wrong."

"We may not doing anything wrong. People are probably bored with my exhibition style."

"Don't say that! Ladybug won an AAM award. There's always a lot of competition for guests during the summer months. The new water park opened."

"Our general visitation numbers were the same. People just didn't go into the exhibit hall."

"Oh, Miriam. What do you think is going to happen?"

"Peter wants to talk about this afternoon. I'm supposed to present ideas for the winter exhibit."

Peter Kotolski was the museum director and had been with the Lampe for fifteen years as assistant director and then director. Well-regarded by the staff, Peter was fair and firm about maintaining Lampe standards.

"This could be your big break," said Miriam.

"Being head curator is too much pressure," said Christine. "I've managed to be assistant curator for eight years. I like that security and hate to move. What are you going to pitch to Peter?"

"I have a radical idea."

"That's good."

"A traveling exhibit."

"Um, we've never had a traveling exhibit. We always use our collection."

"That's why it's a radical idea. I saw some interesting examples at conferences this year. The National Archives is launching a new exhibition of photographs of the National Parks. The state university museum studies program created an exhibition about David Olson, the local nature artist. That exhibition has photographs, paintings, and DVD interviews. Both will cost about thirty-five hundred dollars to rent. We rarely have photos or paintings on display, so either exhibition will be different."

"Um, I'm not sure if Peter and the board will be happy with those ideas. They didn't even want to borrow the ladybug pin from Mrs. Gunderson, and she didn't even charge a fee."

"That was jewelry. We had to build a custom case and obtain additional insurance. We don't have to build anything or pay for a separate insurance policy with these exhibitions. This idea is totally unexpected. Peter and the board will be surprised."

"Will it be a good surprise or a bad surprise?"

"That's for them to decide."

As the meeting continued, Christine's nervousness increased. Was Miriam burned out? Had she given up? Did she already know she was fired and suggesting an easy solution while a search was undertaken? Christine knew that Miriam's meeting with Peter would be a turning point.

The Proposal

Miriam usually had a two-year plan for exhibitions. Last year, Peter told her to focus on one year. She presumed from that instruction that her tenure was coming to an end. The subsequent exhibition failures didn't help. Miriam didn't know if Peter and the board already planned to fire her at the end of the current year or were placing her on some type of secret probation. She tried to ignore her suspicions while crafting her plans. The thought nagged. As she planned the winter exhibition, Miriam decided to propose a new course of action. She felt that the Lampe valued novelty over education and reviewed her most novel or radical options. The National Archives exhibitions impressed her and would help her place the Lampe within a national context, moving away from the board's hyperlocal focus. Reviewing materials from another institution could provide inspiration and other points of view. Miriam had seen several of the state university exhibitions and was impressed with their multimedia options. Supporting young professionals was also important to her.

As Miriam entered Peter's office, she knew her proposal could result in immediate dismissal. She also suspected that dismissal would come sooner or later. She and Peter began by reviewing the guest surveys.

"It's a puzzler," said Peter. "No one disliked the exhibitions, but they didn't love them. I had my doubts about the ladybugs. It was really well-done and different from past exhibitions."

"Thank you," said Miriam. "Predicting exhibition performance is hard. I never would have thought that *Ferns of the Forest* would be our biggest success. The design was beautiful. Karl did an amazing job writing the labels."

"The team does great work executing the visions of the different leaders. They are very talented."

"Yes."

"So what's your proposal for winter?"

"We should do something the Lampe has never done before in its almost hundred-year history."

"The board will be pleased to hear that."

"I am proposing renting either one or two traveling exhibitions. The National Archives is mounting a new exhibition of photographs of National Parks. The state university has a David Olson exhibition. Each costs thirty-five hundred dollars, which is less than our typical exhibition, so we could do both. Each provides a different way to explore nature—through the eyes of the photographer and the artist. We've never produced an art-based exhibit before, so we could attract a new group of visitors."

"Displaying photos and pictures isn't serious scholarship. This seems lazy."

"Both exhibitions come with educational materials. Artists have worked with scientists for decades. Frank Netter's illustrations are still prized by medical students and doctors. Audubon catalogued American birds with scholarship and painting. Both scientists and artists rely on observational skills in their work."

"We aren't an art museum. We're a nature museum. Our exhibitions must include nature—real nature—not pictures of nature. We have a large collection, most of which hasn't been displayed. What about the seashells?"

"Since we aren't in a coastal community, I've had difficulty thinking of an exhibit for them."

"This is disappointing. I expected more from you. Have you given up?"

"Have you given up on me?"

Peter was surprised that Miriam directly confronted him. Past curators simply did their job until dismissed.

"What makes you say that?" asked Peter.

"You reduced the timeframe for the exhibition schedule plan, and I am in the three- to five-year danger zone. Board members don't talk to me at events. If it's time for me to move on, that's fine. Be honest about it. Regardless, I think a traveling exhibition is the right choice for the winter exhibit."

"I'm not planning any immediate staff changes. The board and I are meeting next week. Please write up your recommendations for our review."

Miriam agreed and left Peter's office. He was unsure about their meeting and did not know how he would present Miriam's recommendations to the board. He did know that her analysis of the situation was accurate. The board's thoughts were unclear. As Miriam and Peter prepare for the meeting, they must answer the following questions:

1. How should the Lampe define the success or failure of exhibitions?
2. How can traveling exhibitions be incorporated into the Lampe's exhibition plan?
3. How is the Lampe's curatorial turnover affecting its staff and exhibitions?

Other questions to consider:

1. How should a museum balance the use of traveling exhibitions versus the exhibitions derived from its own collection?
2. What is the board's role in exhibition planning? Does that role vary based on the size of the museum?
3. How should Peter have responded to Miriam's question about her employment status?

CASE 2: PERSKE HISTORY MUSEUM

As Judith Jennings, curator of the Perske History Museum, prepares her recommendations for upcoming exhibitions, Membership Director Ryan Anderson proposes that the public vote to select the next exhibition. Judith disagrees, believing that the curatorial department's expertise is essential to the selection process. Both present their opinions to Museum Director Edie St. John for a final decision.

Museum Background

Located in Bridgetown, population three hundred thousand, the Perske History Museum connects local history with national history—presenting Bridgetown as a typical American city. When John Perske founded the museum in 1889, he interpreted the city's name literally and sought thematic or intellectual bridges between groups of people. Subsequent board members and museum directors used Perske's philosophy as their mission and created programs and exhibitions with underlying themes of connection or linkage.

The people of Bridgetown supported the Perske with annual visitation of fifty thousand and a robust slate of members and donors. The Perske embraced social media and was the first museum in its region to have Facebook and Instagram accounts. Each month, the marketing staff selected its favorite guest photo to highlight via the Perske's various social media accounts. The behind-the-scenes tours always sold out.

The Perske staff sought opportunities to deepen the connection between the museum and its guests. Judith Jennings, the curator, participated in all those activities and asked the curatorial staff to blog about their favorite objects in the collection. When Judith and the curatorial team crafted exhibition proposals, they reviewed guest feedback, current sociopolitical news topics, and historical events. Judith then presented three exhibition proposals to Edie St. John, the museum director, for final approval.

Judith's Presentation

Judith and Edie met every other week. Edie preferred to be surprised about the exhibition proposals, in order to provide an honest, immediate reaction.

"This is our most diverse set of proposals," said Judith.

"Really?" said Edie. "You've been here for twenty years and never said that before."

"We have two proposals that we have worked on for a few years. We felt that they are now ready to be presented. We are also approaching the fiftieth anniversary of 1968."

"I thought we had decided to do the 1968 exhibition regardless."

"That version is multimedia and virtual. We are working on the website and have the clearances for the local news footage. This additional exhibition is titled *1968: The Year of Revolution* and will explore social and cultural changes. One room will have a curtain partition. One side will play early to mid-1960s music and have mannequins dressed for that period. The other side will play the psychedelic songs that emerged in 1967/1968 and have appropriately dressed mannequins. Guests will experience the cultural shifts using the two universals of culture: music and clothes."

After Judith and Edie reviewed the details of the 1968 proposal, Judith presented the second proposal.

"*Jeweler's Row: Art vs. Industry* examines Bridgetown's jewelry industry, the contribution of immigrants, and the national reputation of our local jewelers," said Judith.

"Haven't we done jewelry?" asked Edie.

"Ten years ago we had an exhibition of Mrs. Louis's jewelry. None of the pieces were locally made or designed. That exhibition connected jewelry with the traveling habits of wealthy Gilded Age Americans. We have never had an exhibition about the local jewelry industry."

"That's surprising. Jewelry was a major industry and continues to be significant. We need to address that oversight."

"Another oversight is birds."

"Birds?"

"Bridgetown was on several key bird migratory routes. Birdwatchers from all over the country came here to view the birds. We have taxidermy birds, bird watcher notebooks, and oral histories from bird watchers. Professor Braun at the university is a world-renowned ornithologist and has agreed to help us."

"My cousin is a bird watcher. They are very passionate. That exhibition could generate national interest. How have you and the curatorial team ranked them?"

"Birds, then jewelry, then 1968. A few staff members felt we might be overemphasizing 1968. We have been trying to work with the university for several years. Professor Braun is very enthusiastic, unlike his colleagues. Jewelry should be done at some point. *Birds* seems to be coalescing."

"Each candidate has its merits. You and the team did an outstanding job this year. I like the variety and the intellectual foundations. I also like the programming and partnership opportunities. Have you talked to Ryan?"

Ryan Anderson was the membership directory. Though Judith appreciated his youthful enthusiasm, she felt that Ryan was not always respectful of curatorial practices and concerns. Judith was still shocked that Ryan had suggested using members to clean artifacts, not Judith's idea of a member benefit.

"I have not discussed the exhibition candidates with Ryan," said Judith. "The proposals are confidential to the curatorial department until I present to you."

"Sorry. Let me clarify. Ryan had an idea about the selection process. Let me call him in."

As Edie asked Ryan to come to her office, Judith grew nervous and could not guess what Ryan might suggest.

Ryan's Idea

Both Edie and Judith had worked at the Perske for twenty years and had held their current positions for almost ten years. Edie's career began in membership and fundraising. She witnessed the generational attitudinal shifts toward museums, giving, and membership. Four years ago, the membership director retired. No one else in the department wanted the job.

Wanting a person who understood millennials, Edie used a corporate search firm to find Ryan, a marketing executive at a tech firm. Ryan was intrigued by the opportunity to grow a community of people who were passionate about a cause. His parents were avid museumgoers, and Ryan enjoyed those visits. Ryan's youthful enthusiasm sometimes enervated older staff members. He was respectful and was learning more about museum procedures. Edie fully supported Ryan and dismissed objections based on his age or the traditional ways of the Perske.

As part of his museum education, Ryan read multiple museum periodicals and became a member of other history museums in different parts of the country. He continuously sought ideas or policies for the Perske. During his tenure, the number of millennial members grew 15 percent. Members in other demographic groups appreciated Ryan's enthusiasm and commitment to customer service. Membership retention was at an all-time high of 90 percent. Ryan thought that Judith would be unenthused about his ideas. He hoped that she would keep an open mind.

"Thanks for coming so quickly," said Edie. "We are reviewing the exhibition proposals, and I want you to share your idea with Judith."

"I can't take the credit for the idea. Other museums have done it," said Ryan. "We'll learn what people are interested in and make them feel part of the process."

"What is the idea?" asked Judith.

"Sorry," said Ryan. "The idea is to ask people to vote for their favorite exhibition idea. Then the museum puts on the exhibit. We get a little market research data and advance enthusiasm. The guests feel connected to the decision-making process."

Judith was not sure how to respond. She knew that the museum needed well-attended exhibitions to thrive. The Perske had always weighted intellectual importance over revenue potential.

"How will the process work?" asked Judith.

"Everything is the same, except the decision-making piece," said Ryan. "The curatorial staff will draft its proposals, which you present to Edie. If you and Edie are happy with the candidates, we poll the people in our database. The winner becomes the next exhibit."

"I like the idea," said Edie. "I am willing to test it with this group of proposals. I did say to Ryan that there could be curatorial issues and we three need to discuss the idea."

"The curatorial staff considers multiple factors in creating and ranking exhibition proposals, including guest feedback. We also consider the relationship opportunities with other entities, as well as past exhibitions. Our context is wider than that of the typical guest, who will vote for what they want to see," said Judith.

"Since you have already vetted the proposals to account for those factors, what's the problem with guests and members participating in the final decision?" asked Ryan.

"The bird proposal is the staff's top choice due to its historical significance and collaborative potential with the university—a collaboration we have sought for years. Popular sentiment would probably prefer jewelry or 1968," said Judith.

"Predicting popular sentiment is difficult," said Ryan. "They might vote for birds. We don't know. What if we weight the vote? The museum has 60 percent, and the guest poll is worth 40 percent. Then you will have veto power. We can publish the results of the guest poll. If the staff chooses a different exhibition, we can explain why."

"I like the veto power idea. We do need a safety net," said Edie. "This proposal set is perfect for a first vote. We have a diverse slate of candidates. The decision will be tough. Why not ask our guests?"

"Are we allowing people to access the entire proposal?" asked Judith.

"No," said Ryan. "We will provide a short descriptive paragraph, which can include why the curatorial staff is proposing the exhibition. Then people will have a better understanding of how an exhibition is planned."

"What do you think, Judith?" asked Edie.

"I am uncomfortable with the idea. I am amenable to the veto proposal. Our exhibitions are integral to our mission and the public's trust," said Judith.

"I respect your opinion," said Edie. "You have raised some good points. I will consider both of your opinions and sleep on it. I will announce my decision tomorrow."

Neither Ryan nor Judith was sure what Edie would decide. Edie had great respect for Judith's opinion, especially regarding curatorial issues. Ryan's ideas had been successful. Edie knew she would have to answer the following questions:

1. Why should the Perske ask guests to vote on exhibition proposals?
2. Should the staff veto be implemented? Why or why not?
3. What other factors should be considered when deciding among the three exhibition proposals?

Other questions to consider:

1. Given the complexity of the exhibition planning process, would virtual or pop-up exhibits be better candidates for guest voting? Why or why not?
2. What are the pros and cons of museums directly soliciting exhibition ideas from guests?
3. How should museums incorporate guest feedback or suggestions into exhibition planning?

CASE 3: QUENTIN HISTORICAL SOCIETY

The Quentin Historical Society sits on five acres of land. Four acres are unused. Curator Pete Lovell proposes creating a prairie on those unused acres to recreate the nineteenth-century iteration of the location and to introduce outdoor tours. Facility Rental Manager Jill Anderson is concerned about the impact on her clients, while Museum Director Marianne Umbdenstock is concerned that the proposal strays from the museum's mission.

Museum Background

The Quentin Historical Society served its eponymous county and was located in its eponymous county seat. In the mid-nineteenth century, the Quentins had settled in the area and built a town. As new waves of settlers arrived, the Quentins founded the historical society as a social club, which then morphed into an historical society.

With an annual visitation of thirty thousand, the Quentin was an attraction, but was less popular than the children's museum and the zoo. Its Italianate style building and acreage made it a popular event rental space. The junior college art department used the space for its lecture series. Wedding planners also suggested the Quentin to their brides.

Most of the land was undeveloped with patches of grass, flowers, and trees. The Quentin had bought the land as it became available for preservation purposes but had never considered creating a plan for the land. A plan was needed to replace some of the museum's life-size dioramas. Created in less culturally sensitive times, guests complained about the portrayals of the inter-actions between Europeans and native peoples. The board voted to remove those dioramas from display. Museum Director Marianne Umbdenstock asked Curator Pete Lovell to remove the dioramas and to propose another permanent exhibit.

The New Exhibit

Pete was celebrating his fifth year as curator. Recruited from a major met-ropolitan natural history museum, he was asked to review and refresh all of the Quentin's permanent exhibits. Board members initially resisted Pete's proposals for a complete redesign, fearing that his changes would upset long-term members and guests. So Pete began by revising labels for all the exhibits and slowly changing the smaller exhibits. Guests responded positively to the refreshes, and the Quentin began receiving more media coverage. As a result, the dioramas were scrutinized more closely by the media and became a divisive issue. Members of the public posted their concerns on newspaper websites. People questioned why the Quentin was repainting the old time apothecary and ignoring the dioramas. Thus, the board voted to remove the dioramas.

When Pete was told that he could remove the dioramas and design a new exhibit, he was very excited and decided to create an exhibit that would tell the stories of all the people who had lived on the prairielands. As he stared out his window and saw the acres of land, Pete had an epiphany: use the land as the platform for the exhibit. The board always talked about developing a cohesive landscape plan for the acreage. Restoring the land to its natural prairie state, as well as including nineteenth-century farmlands, would transport guests back to the time of the Quentins's arrival. Representatives from local tribes had already contacted Pete about creating programs and educational materials to share their stories. Tools and equipment from the Quentins's barn were in the collection. Photos of the barn could be used to rebuild it. Guests could time travel by walking through the prairie, visiting the barn and other structures, and then entering the main museum building. Pete began sketching his plan on a map of the grounds.

Jill's Concerns

Pete was so engrossed with his sketch that he didn't notice when Jill Anderson, the facility rental manager, entered his office.

"Hey, Pete," said Jill. "Did that board tour decide on a start time?"

"Huh? Oh, yeah. 4:30. Is that okay for you?" said Pete.

Pete personally conducted tours for board members. This particular tour might have overlapped with one of Jill's events. Jill did not like anything to disrupt her events or her ability to generate revenue.

"Yeah, the tables will be delivered. They'll be lined up against the wall. The board has been very happy with the rental revenue, so it shouldn't be an issue," said Jill.

"We can call it a special behind the scenes tour," said Pete.

"Sure. What's with the map?"

"I am working on an idea for the new permanent exhibit, incorporating the outdoor space. It solves our exhibition and landscaping problems."

"I rent that space."

"The plans won't affect your rentals. If anything people may be more interested in the space."

"We'll see."

Pete was a bit concerned. Jill fought to get her way. Since two of her cousins were board members, she usually prevailed. That afternoon Pete received a call from Marianne Umbdenstock, the museum director.

Marianne's Questions

Pete went to Marianne's office and explained his plan.

"My initial thought is that this plan expands our interpretive opportunities and incorporates the land. We can tell a fuller story," said Pete.

"We're not a nature museum. Developing land or doing land tours falls outside our mission. How expensive will the land redevelopment be?" asked Marianne.

"The Quentins were farmers who bought the land from local tribes. The particularly problematic dioramas depict those interactions. We are moving people from an indoor display to an outdoor interactive. I just thought of the idea this morning, so I haven't had time to develop a budget or an interpretive plan. This is really about Jill, isn't it?" asked Pete.

"Yes, she is concerned about her ability to rent the space. We generate 60 percent of our rental revenue from outdoor usage. The cousin front has been calm. I'd like to keep it that way."

"Jill was the one who almost cost us our nonprofit status because of her aggressive advertising for weddings and her refusal to have the docents provide a five-minute intro at functions. I was the only person who objected when she announced her billboard plan at the staff meeting."

"Yes. The previous museum director was fired, not Jill. I'm not opposed to your proposal. As you said, you are still drafting it. I'm neutral. I'm suggesting that you anticipate and address Jill's objections in your proposal."

"I take that to mean that I should develop a revenue projection for Jill."

"If you are passionate about your proposal, presenting a revenue projection would be wise. First develop the proposal with a budget and interpretive plan for our next one-on-one. If the proposal is sound, then move onto the revenue projection. At the next staff meeting, you can present sketches, the proposal, and revenue projections. Do revenue projections for rentals, tours, and programs. Make it all encompassing."

"Alright," said Pete. "Anything else?"

"Not now," said Marianne.

As Pete returned to his office, he indulged in a moment of anger about the unfairness of the situation. He decided that the moment was right for this proposal. If the budget was reasonable, Pete would also be prepared to answer the following questions:

1. Why should the Quentin use the land to replace the dioramas?
2. Is reconstructing the barn appropriate?
3. How else might the dioramas be used?

Other questions to consider:

1. What should be the procedure or timeline for the curatorial staff to present their proposals to other staff?
2. How should a museum director balance the need for rental revenue and the institution's nonprofit status?

3. If one staff member has a special relationship with the board, how can
   other staff members ensure their ability to work effectively?

EPILOGUE

Guests are the common thread among these three studies: their reactions,
their feedback, and their interpretations of issues. Guests of the Lampe Nature
Museum expect exciting, innovative programs; guests of the Perske History
Museum may have the opportunity to vote on exhibition proposals; guests
of the Quentin Historical Society are concerned about the portrayal of native
peoples in dioramas.

That intersection of guest reactions and museum goals (individual departments and the museum as a whole) must be navigated to design a successful
exhibition. As you answer the questions in these cases, ask yourself if you
are considering the guest's point of view and if your answers would change
by incorporating that point of view.

Chapter 6

Programs and Education

INTRODUCTION

Programs and Education departments inspire and edify guest curiosity. While exhibitions may receive more attention, programs and educational activities create opportunities for guests to interact one-on-one with museum staff and subject matter experts, as well as to expand their knowledge and appreciation of a subject. These personal interactions could inspire a guest to become a museum professional, a member, an educator, a collector, or a donor.

This chapter features three case studies exploring:

- Programs and Education's contributions to mission fulfillment;
- the roles and responsibilities of Programs and Education personnel;
- criteria used to evaluate success; and
- partnerships to attract new audiences or to provide specific expertise for guests.

Budget and content concerns are omnipresent. Each institution must also decide their program and education philosophy. Are Programs and Education integral to the institution and on the same level as exhibitions? Are Programs and Education equally important? What are the content responsibilities for each department? Until these philosophical questions are answered, strategic and tactical issues are unresolvable. As you develop solutions to the questions asked at the end of each case study, consider your personal answers to these questions and your institution's Programs and Education priorities.

CASE 1: BARTON CHILDREN'S MUSEUM

The Barton Children's Museum is hiring a new assistant program director. Nick Dashell, the program director, needs this new hire to help him turn around declining program attendance. The top two candidates represent two different solutions to that problem. Elizabeth Stuart is a young program manager with innovative ideas. Lily Fulbright is a mid-career program manager with experience at children's museums. Museum Director Myrna Chandler must decide if innovation or experience is the answer to the Barton's problems.

Museum Background

The Barton Children's Museum was founded in 1961. Its original mission was to educate children about science. That mission eventually broadened to educating children in research and exploration. Flight simulators, dinosaur digs, and construction sites were perpetually popular interactives. The new 3D printer allowed the Barton to create engineering and design programs.

Well-regarded by the community, the Barton's staff was surprised by the 1–3 percent annual declines in attendance for the past five years. Lexington was a thriving community with a growing number of children. The demographics favored attendance increases. Guest surveys revealed that some attendees regarded the Barton as little more than an indoor playground, good for rainy days. Other comments focused on the ages of the staff members and guides. Parents were concerned that the older staff was either out of touch with current technology trends or would be physically incapable of managing children. Since no incident had occurred to support any of those comments, the staff initially considered them an aberration. The repetition of the comments and the continual attendance declines now forced the Barton to address the issue.

A New Assistant Program Director

When Anne Lockwood, the assistant program director, had to resign because her husband was transferred, Nick Dashell, the program director, and Myrna Chandler, the museum director, agreed that Anne's replacement should be an outside hire with diverse program experience. Nick also believed that the hire should be extroverted and enthusiastic. Myrna wanted someone who could stay within budget.

Since Anne was remaining in Lexington to pack up her house, she agreed to help Nick with the interviews. They interviewed candidates over the phone in round one and then invited four candidates for an in-person interview and to run a program. The final two candidates would then be interviewed by Myrna.

Lily Fulbright was the first finalist. With fifteen years' experience, Lily had worked at two other children's museums which had faced similar issues. She was a skilled negotiator who obtained equipment and materials at the lowest possible price. As a former kindergarten teacher, she had a deep knowledge of child development and inspired confidence from parents. Children were fascinated with her ability to whistle bird calls.

Elizabeth Stuart, the second finalist, had five years of professional experience at a railroad museum. Originally hired as an assistant to the program coordinator, Elizabeth had been promoted every year and currently managed the children's programs. Attendance at Elizabeth's programs increased every year, and she was also skilled at convincing parents to become museum members. Her charisma attracted parents and children.

Nick arranged for Lily and Elizabeth to meet Myrna. He and Anne both agreed that either candidate would do an excellent job. Lily would contribute her experiences at different museums and in the classroom. Elizabeth had success designing and implementing successful programs. Neither Nick nor Anne was sure which candidate Myrna would prefer.

Myrna and Lily

Myrna herself was unsure about how to solve the attendance problem. She was sure that the board was becoming impatient with the lack of a solution, especially after reading the demographic study. Staff changes could be imminent, including a change of museum director. Myrna was confident that the current staff could uncover a solution and believed that a new voice could inspire creativity or provide a different perspective. She was eager to meet both candidates.

Myrna met Lily first and was impressed with her administrative acumen and warm nature.

"I'm sure Nick and Anne told you about our attendance issue," said Myrna.

"Yes," said Lily. "I was a bit unclear if the issue is program specific or museum wide."

"Both. Initially, program attendance was flat, while museum attendance declined slowly. Now both are consistently declining."

"Are other cultural institutions in Lexington facing the same issue?"

"The art museum is doing very well. The history museum is flat. The director retired last year, and the new permanent director has yet to be hired. We started working with a local children's theater group. Their attendance has increased, so we are hoping that partnership will help us. Have you worked with partners? Were the relationships beneficial?"

"We work with an amazing puppet theater troop that puts on a show and teaches puppetry to children. They learn how to develop a character and then manufacture their puppet. We also have a magician who is incredibly temperamental, but crazy popular with guests. I make sure to have a full bottle of aspirin available when I have to deal with him."

"How is he difficult?"

"Administratively, he forgets to sign or mail his contract. He also lost his check and accused us of not paying him. From a performance standpoint, he continually pitches illusions involving fire. We have a firm anti-fire policy."

"As do we. What are your impressions of our program slate?"

"At first glance, the programs are very creative and interactive with a good variety of subjects. As I analyzed the programs for age cohorts, I discovered that the programs skewed toward preschoolers and fifth to sixth graders. Identifying the appropriate age group from some of the descriptions was difficult. I personally like to state the age group on the collateral—makes it easier for the parents. Ideally, I like to have a program for each age group per program schedule. The availability of partners can impact that ideal. At the end of the year, we should have a relatively even distribution among the ages."

"Doesn't that require developing and administering a lot of different programs?"

"Not really. We can take one concept and adapt it to the different ages. Our local university has a grad program in childhood development. Students volunteer to adapt our programs. We're lucky in that respect. Otherwise, we would not be able to adapt all the programs."

Myrna and Lily finished their conversation. Myrna was impressed with Lily's deep understanding of children and her observations about the age cohorts. Myrna knew Nick and his team did create different tiers of programs, but they had never really analyzed their offerings by age group.

Myrna and Elizabeth

Elizabeth was very charismatic. Myrna could sense her presence outside the door. Elizabeth's enthusiasm and friendly nature would attract parents. Myrna was pleasantly surprised at Elizabeth's highly analytical approach to program development.

"Your career path at the railroad museum is impressive," said Myrna.

"Thank you," said Elizabeth. "We have a great team. The director is very supportive. I wasn't sure if children's programs were right for me. I don't have a teaching background or degree, but I love it. I have taken some education and childhood development classes, which have helped me create programs and materials for different grades. The teachers at the local elementary school review materials and make suggestions, too."

"Railroads are a very specific topic. How do you develop new programs?"

"I look at the railroads from three perspectives: transportation, shipping, and technology. How do railroads compare to boats? What do railcars carry? How do trains work? Then I research what kids are interested in. What are popular games or books or toys? What are the themes of the popular items? Last year, kids were really into how things worked, so we created programs about the invention of the steam engine and the building of railroad tracks. Two years ago, they were interested in building virtual worlds. Our programs allowed them to build their version of the transcontinental railroad."

"How do you identify their interests?" asked Myrna.

"I talk to them when they visit the museum. I also look to see what books or games they are carrying. I talk to the public librarians and people who work in toy stores. Of course teachers know what the kids are into," said Elizabeth.

"How long does it take you to develop a program? Aren't you always a year behind?"

"We run three children's programs per quarter. One is always a classic. Another one might also be a repeat. One is always new. I have a budget of a few hundred dollars per program, so my primary issue is limited dollars, rather than time."

"We are a children's museum. Are you confident that your experience at the railroad museum has prepared you for an assistant program director position here?"

"Yes. Because the railroad museum has a much smaller staff, you learn at a really fast pace or fail. I have created twelve original programs in the last two years and have been created with recruiting thirty-five new family-level memberships. Children's programming is my passion. This opportunity will help me hone my new skills. Nick will be a great mentor. I would appreciate the opportunity to build on my past success."

Myrna was impressed with Elizabeth's ability to generate multiple revenue streams and to reach out to different groups of people to understand children and to create relationships for her museum. She understood why Nick and Anne liked both candidates.

Nick and Myrna Meet

"So?" asked Nick.

"This is the toughest hiring decision I think I have ever made," said Myrna.

"I wish we could hire them both. Lily is the consummate profession who could hit the ground running. Elizabeth is a diamond in the rough, who has her finger on the pulse of kids."

"Unfortunately, we can't hire them both. The board and the guests will also like both of them. We may be here a while."

Myrna and Nick decided to rate each candidate's ability to meet the specific criteria in the job description. In the process of selecting their choice, they answered the following questions:

1. Is creative program development or administrative acumen more important for the Barton? Why or why not?
2. Which of the candidates' past experiences can directly address the Barton's attendance decline?
3. What are the risks and benefits of hiring each candidate?

Other questions to consider:

1. Under what circumstances should a museum hire a less experienced, very talented professional?
2. Should the program department be given attendance goals? Why or why not?
3. How might a children's museum collaborate with other educational institutions to develop programs?

CASE 2: NORMAN SCIENCE MUSEUM

A Norman Science Museum board member reads an article about an academic art museum, which combined its programs and education departments. He asks Museum Director Paula Eastman to consider a similar arrangement at the Norman. Paula discusses the idea with Education Director Marjorie Oswald and Programs Director Diane Edwards and attempts to define the museum's point of view about such an action.

Museum Background

Until the late 1990s, the Norman Science Museum had been a medium-sized science museum that focused on its marine life and oceanography collections. The dot.com boom enabled local entrepreneurs to earn and spend vast fortunes. The Norman was seen as a vehicle to share technology knowledge among the community. A new wing was constructed; staff expanded; and the budget increased to three million dollars per year.

The public responded enthusiastically, and annual attendance ballooned to one hundred thousand people per year. School field trips instigated additional visits. The children especially enjoyed the interactives and learning activities about hurricanes and typhoons. Located in a coastal city, the Norman's mission had always involved expanding knowledge of the ocean, its creatures, and the climate. The .com dollars allowed the Norman to install virtual reality storm simulators. The Norman's educational materials and activities were well-regarded and award-winning.

Its programs were primarily created for adults and included special lectures, concerts, and book clubs. While the Education Department worked with the curatorial staff on exhibitions, Programs were more independent and attracted new audiences to the Norman. Diane Edwards, the program director, and Marjorie Oswald, the education director, had a cordial working relationship. Diane was bothered that Education had a much larger budget than Programs. Marjorie was pragmatist, who maintained her composure at all times.

The Conversation

Board member Arnold Simmons came to the Norman for a sneak preview of the upcoming sea otter exhibition. Arnold was the CFO for a major tech firm and provided financial expertise to the Norman. He rarely offered an opinion about museum governance, but he avidly read the articles about museums that Paula sent to the board. Since he didn't understand the fundamentals of the museum industry, Arnold typically deferred to Paula's opinions. He was intrigued by an article about a reopened art museum and wanted to discuss it with Paula.

"Am I interrupting?" asked Arnold.

"No, please come in," said Paula. "I was actually going to look for you and invite you to lunch. I'd love to hear your thoughts about the exhibit."

"Those otters are pretty gosh darn cute. I can already hear my daughter's squeals of delight."

"A third-grade class saw us moving some of the panels. I didn't know that little girls could scream that loudly."

"My ear drums are still recovering from her first concert. Next time, I will bring ear plugs. Unfortunately, I can't stay for lunch. I would like to talk about the art museum article for a minute."

"Sure. I thought the rearrangement of the floors by theme was interesting. We should think about that when we expand the ecosystem galleries. Visitors like the timelines, but they also want to see the species interact."

"You and Joyce understand that better than I. Actually, I was interested in the merger of the Education and Programs Departments into one entity; seemed very logical. The programs are also educational."

"Some museums do combine the two due to resource constraints or museum missions. A college art museum doesn't have the volume of school field trips that we do. Other museums work closely with local school systems and need an education staff who are well versed in Common Core and state standards. Other museums have collections that skew toward adults or college age students, so they focus on programs. Most of our visitors are families or school groups, so education is key. Since a lot of researchers use our collections, we like to have them lecture about their findings. Our concert series introduce a number of people to the museum. Maintaining separate departments has worked well for us."

"There could be duplication of effort. Diane's programs always make money. Education might benefit from her leadership."

"That's an interesting thought. Programs are designed to break even or generate revenue. Education is not, so the comparison isn't exactly apples to apples."

"I think we should explore the idea at the next board meeting. Always good to turn the magnifying glass on yourself," said Arnold.

"Change is a constant," said Paula. "I'll talk to Diane and Marjorie to come up with a point of view and additional examples of other museums with a similar system."

"Great. I appreciate that. Thank you."

After Arnold left, Paula considered the pros and cons of merging Education and Programs. Because Arnold rarely advanced a course of action and was very well-respected by the entire board, Paula knew that the board would seriously consider his proposal and probably approve it. She called Marjorie and Diane to her office to discuss the situation.

The Museum Staff Meets

Paula shared Arnold's thoughts with Diane and Marjorie.

"Arnold is really intrigued by this idea," said Paula. "It appeals to his love of efficiency. He could convince the board to consolidate the departments. I am not in favor of consolidation because each department has unique audiences and different workflows. I don't see a lot of overlap. If the two of you are amenable to consolidation, then I will reconsider my position."

"Who would be in charge of new department?" asked Diane.

Marjorie laughed.

"Arnold thought you should be in charge because programs generate revenue, and he thinks educational activities should also earn money. I did explain that Education is not and should not be a revenue generating department," said Paula.

"No worries," said Marjorie. "I agree that merging the departments is not a good idea for the reasons you mentioned. As one department, we would be at cross purposes."

"I would have access to additional staff," said Diane. "Programs is always understaffed."

"Because you have access to more volunteers and docents than Marjorie," said Paula. "Do you think that the two departments should merge?"

"I don't have time to manage my own programs, much less someone else's," said Diane.

"Setting aside the daily practicalities, in theory, do you think that the Programs and Education Departments should be combined?" asked Paula.

"Combining the two departments would probably create some efficiencies. We already have cross-departmental meetings. The budgets and the staff are separate. I wouldn't have a problem reporting to a new person who would be in charge of both departments," said Diane.

"That won't happen," said Paula. "If the departments are combined, the board will expect budget and staff decreases. One of the two of you would be the new department head. Due to the volume of school visits, the program staff would be more likely to be pulled to support education, rather than the reverse."

"I assume this suggestion came from the art museum article," said Marjorie.

Paula nodded.

"Combining departments won't increase budget or staff," said Marjorie. "If Education has to justify its existence via revenue, we may as well eliminate the department now. I think if we compare our attendance, budget, and stats for programs and educational activities to institutions that combine Programs and Education, we will see that the volumes aren't comparable. I have a hard time believing that a college art museum's numbers, especially attendance, are comparable to ours."

"The budget could be close. Art is expensive. I do agree that attendance and program stats will be quite dissimilar. Diane?" said Paula.

"A numerical comparison would be helpful," said Diane.

"Okay," said Paula. "We each have different groups of colleagues and resources. If we can each get data from one to three other museums that have combined Programs and Education, we can analyze that data. I'll call the art museum in the article. As of now, is it safe to say that Marjorie and I oppose the proposal, and, Diane, you support it?"

"I'm undecided," said Diane.

"Okay," said Paula. "The board meets in two weeks. Let's spend a week gathering data and then meet to analyze findings. Just so there is no misunderstanding, this topic should not be discussed with anyone. I do not want panic over an idea that has not been officially presented to the board. The board might consider more exploration of the idea or immediately decide against it. Understood?"

Marjorie and Diane nodded their assent. As the three women began their research, they knew the board would ask the following questions:

1. What are the benefits and drawbacks of merging the Programs and Education Departments at the Norman?
2. How should Paula explain the different revenue and mission support responsibilities of Programs versus Education?
3. How do the educational activities and programs at a science museum differ from those at an art museum? Or other types of museums?

Other questions to consider:

1. What other data should Paula, Marjorie, and Diane collect?
2. What other responses or tactics could Paula have used when Arnold suggested merging the departments?
3. If the departments are merged, who should be the new director? Why or why not?

CASE 3: STONE-PARKER PLANETARIUM

The Stone-Parker Planetarium and the Science Department of the Isaacson Community College have an informal relationship that allows Isaacson students to use the Stone-Parker's observatory and that uses Isaacson professors as lecturers and consultants for the Stone-Parker. Eric Garrison, the Isaacson liaison, proposes joint adult education classes. Stone-Parker Education Manager Kyle Stanley is interested but uncertain about the ethics and logistics of such an arrangement.

Museum Background

The Stone-Parker Planetarium evolved from an observatory built by George Stone in 1908 to view Halley's Comet in 1910 into a planetarium in the 1950s. John Parker purchased the observatory in 1942 to watch for German war planes during World War II. Upon his death in 1955, Parker's will created the Stone-Parker Planetarium, which consisted of the observatory and Parker's house. Over time, the house was remodeled into an open floor plan and with an additional wing.

The declining interest in the space race and the end of the Cold War translated into decreasing attendance and a very small budget. Sharon Hayes, the planetarium director and curator, was the only full-time employee. One part-time employee managed sales and membership. Kyle Stanley, the other part-time employee, was the educator and coordinated group tours. Volunteers led tours and helped with special projects.

Sharon and Kyle tried to form relationships with other museums and science groups. Isaacson Community College was the only institution that reciprocated that interest. Partnering with the Stone-Parker gave the Isaacson unique access to the observatory, which sparked student interest and created internship opportunities. Both institutions benefited from the arrangement.

The Idea

Every quarter, Kyle and Eric Garrison, the Isaacson's liaison to the Stone-Parker, had lunch. They reviewed statistical data and any issues that had arisen.

"We were very happy," said Kyle. "It was a great group of kids this semester who were very respectful of the equipment. No one left cans or chip bags in the observatory. Thirty people came to Professor Randall's lecture. I think this was our best semester yet."

"We heard from a couple of kids who transferred to the state university. Their work at the observatory put them ahead of the other astronomy students. One was given a TAship," said Eric.

"That's terrific," said Kyle. "These success stories are really helping. Our attendance actually increased 1 percent last year."

"Why so excited about 1 percent?"

"We're usually barely able to maintain the same attendance from year to year. We haven't had an actual increase in fifteen years."

"If you're that excited about 1 percent, you may not be able to handle my proposition."

"What do you mean?"

"We're expanding our adult education offerings. The observatory is a great resource, so we want to add astronomy classes to the schedule."

"That sounds great! I'm sure we can work out a reasonable way for you to use the building. Technically, I think it would be a facility rental. Sharon will know how to do it. Thank you for thinking of us."

"No, no. You don't understand."

"What?"

"We want you to teach the classes. We don't have enough staff to expand that much, so we are talking to partners who have expertise and their own spaces. They'll run the classes in their facilities, and we'll handle the admin and registration. The course fee will be split between the two of us, probably 50–50. Rita who runs the pottery studio is in, so is Herb at the book store."

"We're a bit different."

"You're an educator. You have those Common Core and state standards packets. You don't even need that for adult education. People would be happy with those demos you do with the students."

"Our education materials and activities support our mission. I don't know if we are allowed to sell our classes."

"Are the museum police going to arrest you?"

"Not just them. I'm not sure if it's ethical."

"Seriously, there are museum police?"

"If you are an accredited museum, then yes. You could lose your accreditation."

"Do you have to shut down?"

"No. Most museums aren't accredited. Planetariums are a different anyway. We aren't accredited by the museum people, and the planetarium people don't have an accreditation."

"So there's no problem."

"I don't know. I've never heard of this type of arrangement. I'll have to talk to Sharon."

The two men continued their lunch. Both were excited about the idea. Kyle tried to think of any other objections to the plan, but couldn't. He was curious about Sharon's reaction.

The Discussion

When Kyle returned to the Stone-Parker, he checked the websites for the International Planetariums Society and the American Alliance of Museums, but couldn't find any guidance for this particular proposal. He also looked for another example of a museum providing adult education classes for a college. He found museum personnel who teach at colleges, but those activities seemed separate from the museum. Kyle then went to Sharon's office and explained the proposition to her.

"Eric is ambitious. He has really shaken up that college for the better," said Sharon. "I like that he thinks of us; so few people want to work with us. Something about this proposal seems . . . wrong, for lack of a better word."

"That was my thought," said Kyle. "We charge admission, tour, and program fees, but we don't really charge for teaching. We have downloadable course packs on our website. We charge a tour fee to school groups who physically come here for demos and use the education packets. That doesn't seem the same as teaching formal classes and charging tuition. Museums that have their own schools do it, but the schools are separate. Maybe it's okay?"

"I really like this idea. It introduces us to new people and brings in more money. It's hard to fulfill your mission when no one comes through the door. Realistically, do we have enough staff to run classes?"

"The classes run six to ten weeks and meet once a week for two hours. I can teach the first class using our comet materials and see how it works."

"Sounds like we are going to do this."

"Based on my research this afternoon, I don't see any reason why we can't. I would feel more comfortable if we both did background research and talked to our colleagues. It's too bad we can't afford association memberships. This opportunity could be a major turning point for us," said Kyle.

"It could be. The main problem is that we don't have the staff or budget to absorb any mistakes. Let's present the opportunity to the board for their feedback," said Sharon.

Kyle and Sharon decided to conduct more research into other museums that might have similar relationships with colleges or universities and how those relationships work. Their presentation to the board answered the following questions:

1. What are the ethical considerations involved in the proposed relationship between the Isaacson and the Stone-Parker?
2. What issues need to be resolved or defined in any contract between the two institutions?
3. Given its limited resources, how will the Stone-Parker be able to teach adult education classes?

Other questions to consider:

1. Which cultural and educational institutions are complementary partners with museums? How can such partnerships benefit both institutions?
2. What other technologies or methods could a museum use to share its educational materials?
3. How do programs and educational activities support a museum's mission?

EPILOGUE

Programs and Education Departments face similar pressures as exhibitions: attendance, revenue, mission execution, and staffing, but can lack the attention or excitement given to a major exhibition. Measuring the success of their efforts can be difficult. As the front line of public interaction, Programs and Education staff have the opportunity to engage and excite guests at a personal level. These three case studies demonstrate how institutions must balance those pressures.

The Barton Children's Museum must decide between an experienced professional or an innovative newcomer to invigorate its programs. The Norman

Science Museum might restructure its organizational chart. The Stone-Parker Planetarium has an interesting partnership opportunity. Each of these organizations is contemplating fundamental strategic decisions that could alter their Programs and Education philosophies. As you craft your responses to the questions, consider how your personal philosophy of the goals for Programs and Education Departments is affecting your answers.

Chapter 7

Community Engagement

INTRODUCTION

Community engagement is a nebulous term that museums may define differently: off-site interaction with the community, issue advocacy, and/or calls to action for the community. The Internet enables people from around the world to utilize a museum's educational materials, view exhibition materials, see programs, and become a member even without physically entering the museum. Virtual museums can interact with people without even having a physical location. Has the world become a museum's community? If a museum focuses on a specific subject, are those subject matter enthusiasts its community? Should a museum consider everyone as a member of its community? Should a museum provide a definition of its community alongside its mission statement? At the very least, as an institution of public trust, a museum is obliged to declare and explain its position on relevant topics and to promote education as a means to resolving differences.

This chapter features three case studies exploring:

- the role of the museum in the community;
- interactions with other organizations;
- supporters' expectations; and
- opportunities outside the museum.

At its core, community engagement is a dialogue between a museum and people. The museum's mission statement declares its goals for educating or inspiring the public to action. The public may turn to a museum for guidance because of its expertise in specific subjects or its reputation as a scholarly institution. When a museum and the public understand the other's goals and capabilities, they can effectively cooperate. As you develop solutions to the questions asked at the end of each case study, consider the gap between your personal responses to the issues and an institution's response.

CASE 1: OWENS VETERAN'S MUSEUM

David Owens was a World War II hero whose home became a museum. Concerned that Owens and the World War II generation are being forgotten, Elk Grove Mayor Bill Thompson is leading a campaign to erect a monument of Owens in the town square. Reaction to the artist's proposed design is negative, with the Owens Family leading the opposition. The mayor, citizens, and Owens Family want Owens Museum Director Tina Dowd to publicly declare the museum's position on the monument. Tina is weighing the museum's civic responsibility and the potential consequences of declaring a position.

Museum Background

World War II fighter pilot David Owens distinguished himself with daring reconnaissance flights over Germany. After his plane was shot down, he evaded German capture and gathered additional intelligence as he returned to Allied lines. When Owens returned home, he spent the rest of his life as an advocate for veterans. After Owens's death in 2000, the town of Elk Grove approached the Owens Family about purchasing Owens's home and turning it into a museum. The Owens Family agreed, with the caveat that the museum focus on veteran advocacy and post-war transition to civilian life. Owens himself always refused special awards or honors, so his family knew that he would not want a shrine to his memory.

Museum Director Tina Dowd and Programs and Curatorial Coordinator Maggie Shubow concentrated on the museum's interpretation and activities around the veteran's return from war, using Owens's story as a segue. The Owens Museum organized Christmas card signings for active duty troops and local veterans, Quilts of Valor presentations, and kissing pillow stitcha-thons, as well as telling the stories of local soldiers. The museum worked with the American Legion and a nearby VA hospital to bring its programs to veterans in other venues.

The museum building itself received relatively few visitors for the twice-per-week tours; program attendance contributed the majority of the five thousand annual visitors. Program fees, donations, and grants supplied the thirty thousand dollar annual budget. Local government officials, the local American Legion president, veterans, and a member of the Owens Family sat on the board. The town and the board appreciated Museum Director Tina Dowd's ability to maintain a neutral position while navigating divisive local and national issues. Tina reminded people that the museum's mission was to educate about and advocate for the veteran returning home, not to pass judgment on the wars.

The Memorial

Elk Grove was a small town, population twenty thousand. Maggie Shubow, the museum's program and curatorial coordinator, had dated the current mayor, Bill Thompson, when both were in high school. Bill's reputation as a back slapper and glad hander began with his election as junior class president.

"Don't worry, Maggie," yelled Bill. "I have plenty of gas in the car."

"I outran you then, and I can outrun you now," replied Maggie.

"You always were a good sport," said Bill. "Can I buy you a cup of coffee?"

"What's up?"

"You're so suspicious."

"You only pay for the coffee when you want something."

Bill laughed. He and Maggie entered the local diner and sat in a booth.

"This must be serious," said Maggie. "You're sitting with your back to the crowd."

"Well, it's important," said Bill. "I've been thinking about legacies. We really aren't doing a good job of honoring our important citizens."

"Depends on what you mean by honoring," said Maggie. "People supported collecting and exhibiting pictures of the mayors in Town Hall. The library collects family papers and genealogy records. We're fulfilling Mr. Owens's wishes."

"Yeah, but we need to do more. We only have two statues in the park, both from the Civil War. We need more public statues."

"Don't you remember what happened when we were in third grade? Mayor Green wanted to install that dog statue. People got upset about the expense, so it never happened."

"What was the deal with the dog?"

"I think it was a fire department dog that found people in burning buildings."

"Exactly! If the statue was there, we would know about the dog. I just came back from a conference where we talked about preserving our local history."

"Wasn't that a tourism conference?"

"Doesn't matter. We need to memorialize our local heroes."

"Meaning?"

"At the conference, I met this artist, Anton Reghy. He does public art and has pieces in almost every major city. He was really interested in David Owens and is working on some sketches."

"Does the Owens Family know?"

"Yeah, I told them as soon as I came back. They aren't happy, but can't do anything."

"The family is highly respected, and some of his friends are still alive."

"Once they see the design, they will be on board. It's very artistic."

"What does that mean?"

"You'll see. I'm having a press conference next week to unveil it. I want you and Tina to come. Your support will be helpful."

"We'd be happy to sit in the audience. The museum isn't involved in the project and hasn't seen the sketches, so we can't support it sight unseen."

"It's really great. You'll want to get in on the ground floor."

"If our support was that important, you would have told us before now."

"Ouch! I need 'yes' people to push this through. You and Tina aren't reliable 'yes' people."

"That is true. We do like to think before forming an opinion."

"Politicians can't let thinking slow them down. Once you see the design, you'll be impressed."

Maggie and Bill finished their coffee. When Bill returned from conferences, he usually had several project proposals—some useful, some not. Maggie wasn't surprised that Bill wanted to erect a David Owens memorial. Other mayors had tried and failed, because David Owens himself led the opposition. Discussion about installing more public art had also occurred without resolution. Maggie was curious to see the design and to observe the subsequent reaction.

The Press Conference

A week later, Maggie and Tina walked over to the Town Hall for the press conference. Word had quickly spread about the proposed Owens Memorial. The Owens Family reserved comment until the press conference. David and Margaret, the Owens's grandchildren, had asked Tina if she or Maggie had seen the design, but Bill was keeping it secret until the press conference. The grandchildren had decided to keep an open mind and evaluate the memorial on its own merits. They were amenable to a statue or fountain in the town park.

Tina was also keeping an open mind, but was concerned. She had reviewed Anton Reghy's work and was surprised that an artist who generally worked in the abstract would be interested in creating a statue. She decided to refrain from any immediate reaction and to reiterate David Owens's wishes if asked.

Given the museum's dependence on donations and town funds, Tina wanted to remain neutral for as long as possible.

"Welcome, welcome," said Bill. "Thank you all, especially the Owens Family for coming. We have a real treat for you. I know everyone is dying to see the design, so let's get to it. I want to introduce our artist Anton Reghy and have him say a few words before the unveiling. Anton?"

"Good morning," said Anton. "I understand that Mr. Owens was not interested in personal aggrandizement. He stood for certain beliefs and ideals. I took that as my inspiration: to create a sculpture of ideas."

Tina and Maggie glanced at each other. The crowd began murmuring. The Owens grandchildren grimaced.

"I know you are wondering how this is possible," continued Anton. "It's a world of connections, circles, pathways surrounding the fire of war. We orbit chaos and carnage."

"Do you think he designed a solar system?" whispered Maggie.

Tina grew pale. The murmuring grew louder. Sensing the crowd's impatience, Anton removed the drapery from the poster board and stood aside. The crowd hushed.

Maggie's interpretation of Anton's comments was somewhat accurate. A spiked ball was surrounded by concentric rings of different shapes and sizes. A chain emerged from the ball and linked the rings. People turned their heads sideways, trying to understand the drawing. Anton began to speak, but Bill interrupted him.

"I know, I know," said Bill. "It's pretty wild. We had to think outside the box here. David Owens was pretty specific about not wanting a statue. So I explained to Anton about how David connected with veterans from all wars and ages, bringing them together, sharing their war experiences. So we have all the circles of veterans around a ball of war."

Everyone in the room turned toward the Owens grandchildren. David's eyes were wide; he couldn't speak. Margaret, mad and teary, stood and left.

David rose and said, "I don't know how to respond. I appreciate that you tried to respect his wishes. His wish was for this money and effort to be spent on veterans." He then left the room.

As the reporters recovered from the surprise, they began asking the crowd for reactions. Tina and Maggie decided to leave. As they returned to the museum, they found David and Margaret at the door.

"What did you think?" asked Margaret.

"I was completely surprised," said Tina. "I never would have thought Bill would propose an abstract piece."

"It's a mockery of my grandfather," said Margaret. "He hated pretense and snobby art. He wanted the people to help veterans, not worship at his shrine."

"We will fight this sculpture," said David. "It's unnecessary and more about Bill than our grandfather. We came here to find out whose side you're on."

"Do you mean personally or as the museum staff?" asked Tina.

"Both, I guess," said David.

"Personally, I respect your grandfather's wishes. He was very clear on the topic. For the museum, the board should craft a public statement for the staff to use. Obviously, I would help the board coalesce around a position," said Tina.

"I'm the board chair, so I'm calling a special meeting tomorrow to discuss a statement opposing this ridiculous object," said Margaret. "Draft a statement to that effect."

"She can't do that," said David. "The board has to discuss the issue and then draft a statement. As mayor, Bill is on the board, along with all the selectmen. We don't know how the selectmen will vote."

"You'll vote for it," said Margaret.

"I'm not officially on the board right now," said David.

"I will invite the board members to a special meeting tomorrow," said Tina. "Everyone expected that we would meet after the press conference and cleared their schedules. They will also have had time to process the information and develop their opinions."

"Fine," said Margaret, as she and David left.

"Nice punt to the board," said Maggie.

"My comments would be inappropriate until the board met anyway," said Tina. "We have a real problem. About half the board are elected officials who want to be reelected and need favors from Bill. The other half are loyal to the Owens Family. We could have a really ugly meeting tomorrow, with the museum being collateral damage."

Maggie and Tina returned to work and tried not to think about the next day's board meeting. Tina knew she would have to help the board answer the following questions:

1. What is the museum's role in the public art discussion?
2. Should the discussion focus on the artistic merits of the proposed sculpture or Mr. Owens's wishes?
3. How should the board craft the public statement?

Other questions to consider:

1. Regardless of the board discussion, what role can individual staff members play in the public discussion?
2. How can Tina mitigate the risk to the museum if the board meeting becomes too contentious?

3. Should Margaret and Bill recuse themselves from the board discussion? Why or why not?

CASE 2: CORBETT ART MUSEUM

The Corbett Art Museum is experiencing a precipitous decline in attendance, including school groups. Visitors complain about rude or snobby staff. Programs consist solely of art lectures. New Museum Director Jerry Agnew is seeking new opportunities for the Corbett and is excited about a potential partnership with a local hospital. Curator Agatha van Milbank is concerned about the time cost for the curatorial staff.

Museum Background

The Corbett Art Museum was founded in 1905 to house the treasures that Cabotstown's elite had acquired during European travels. As the *nouveau riche* of the Gilded Age became the upper middle class of the Progressive Era, they could not afford to maintain their treasures and decided that a museum was the best solution. The Corbett was initially a members-only museum that opened its doors to the general public with a steep admission fee in 1943. School groups were allowed to visit the Corbett in the hopes that the art would prove uplifting.

As the post-war art world grew populist, the Corbett unofficially ceased collecting twentieth-century art and focused on pre-twentieth-century art. It had a fine collection of religious art and portraits of famous Americans, which were less interesting to the modern and post-modern audience. The aggregation of the multiple small endowments from the founders insulated the Corbett from the subsequent attendance decline. When attendance plummeted from fifty thousand people per year to twenty thousand people per year, the board decided a change was needed.

Hiring Jerry Agnew as the museum director was the first step. Jerry had been an assistant curator at the Corbett fifteen years prior. He then became the curator of Renaissance art at a larger metropolitan museum and was subsequently promoted to deputy director. The Corbett approached Jerry about the museum director position, reasoning that a former staff member would have more credibility with the current staff.

Jerry was excited to return to the Corbett. He left because of the "fuddy-duddyness." He heard that the new Program Director Anne Roberts was very good and had ideas about reaching out to the community. He suspected that some of the long-term staff would be less enthusiastic and was especially concerned about Curator Agatha van Milbank. Agatha believed her life's work was to protect the collection from danger. She welcomed scholars to view the collection, but was less enthusiastic about the general public. Agatha was antagonistic to most people, but her family was one of the museum's original founding families. She was well-respected in the larger curatorial community.

Anne Roberts, the program director, began working at the Corbett six months prior to Jerry's return. She moved to Cabotstown when her husband was transferred there. The board leapt at the opportunity to hire someone with her extensive programming experience. The Corbett's programs were generally acknowledged as limited and boring. Curators lectured about works from the collection. Special events for exhibitions were nonexistent. Anne began by inviting art historians to lead discussions about the collection and the art movements represented in the collection. Initially unenthused, Agatha discovered that the art historians attracted a respectful audience who appreciated the Corbett's collection.

The Request

As Jerry was waiting in line at the coffee shop, someone tapped on his shoulder.

"Aren't you Jerry Agnew?" asked the woman.

"Yes," replied Jerry. "How can I help you?"

"My name is Karen Simmons. I'm the outreach director for the Imblum Hospital."

"Nice to meet you."

"Likewise. I wanted to talk to you about coordinating some programs. We have several long-term care wards for adults and children. We have an art therapist who works with those folks. At other hospitals, she partnered with museums to bring art programs to the hospital. I was wondering if you are interested in working something out. Oh, Agatha is my second cousin, so I understand if it's too difficult."

Jerry laughed, "I appreciate her passion. She does represent important points of view. We are trying to reach new audiences in different ways, though."

"Yes, I attended Professor Kyle's lecture. That's what inspired me to talk to you. Identifying diseases using people's portraits is fascinating. The *Lancet* has a similar series. Our doctors love it."

"I'll talk to Anne Roberts, our program director, and set up a time for the three of us to meet. Thank you for reaching out—literally and figuratively."

Karen and Jerry exchanged business cards. As Jerry walked to the Corbett, he considered several possibilities. Slide shows would be easy. All the exhibitions from the past five years already had electronic presentations that could be adapted with the help of the art therapist. Some of the art historians were open to other types of programs. Jerry was sure that Anne would leap at the opportunity.

Jerry and Anne Meet

After checking his messages, Jerry went to Anne's office and shared his conversation with Karen.

"What a great opportunity," said Jerry. "We should be able to use existing materials and dip our toes into off-site programs with minimal cost. The hospital has a media team, so we might even get some positive press coverage."

"We should give family memberships to the kids," said Anne. "We really need to jump start membership, and a museum visit would be a nice break for the families. Money is so tight when your child is sick, too."

"That's a great idea."

"There are lots of possibilities. We can start with the slideshows and coordinate with the art therapist. Do you think we could use the deaccessioned pieces?"

"It would definitely be a more educational use of them. Let's talk to Agatha."

The Corbett had a collection of deaccessioned objects. Some were pieces that had been identified as fakes; others were subpar works initially accessioned as part of larger collections. The board refused to sell the objects. The pieces instead formed a type of lending library. Museum members or major donors would borrow the objects for personal use. The lending fees provided a steady revenue stream. The curatorial staff managed the collection.

Agatha's Point of View

Jerry and Anne explained the hospital opportunity to Agatha, including the potential use of the deaccessioned works.

"Is the curatorial staff expected to present all these talks? Our time is tightly scheduled, especially during exhibition installations," said Agatha.

"The program staff or the art therapist will most likely give the talks," said Anne.

"So you want to take our work and use it," said Agatha. "How are you going to answer questions?"

"We can adapt the slides, similar to how we create the education materials based on the exhibition labels and curatorial slideshows," said Anne. "We can write down any unanswerable questions and share the answers later. I anticipate that these will be multi-session events, so we will have time for research and dialogue."

"What if the slides can't be adapted?" asked Agatha.

"The art therapist is experienced in such things, so adaptation shouldn't be a problem," said Jerry. "The question now is do we want to participate. If yes, then how."

"If people are interested in art and the interpretation, they should come to the museum," said Agatha.

"Ideally, yes," said Jerry. "We don't live in an ideal world. The hospital patients are in long-term care wards, so they can't come to the museum. Other people may not know that they are interested in our collections until they see the pieces. They won't walk through our front door because they don't know what we have. I'd rather engage people with educational activities than a TV commercial."

"Yes, I agree," said Agatha. "Are you expecting us to transport objects off-site?"

"Not items from the official collection," said Jerry. "The insurance company would not be happy. As a museum goer, blank spaces on the walls are annoying."

"We thought using the deaccessioned pieces for off-site programs makes sense. They move around all the time and aren't that important," said Anne.

"The pieces are important as institutional history," said Agatha. "Though they are transported more frequently than the accessioned pieces, a curator still accompanies the object and supervises the installation. Art must be handled properly. Hospitals have all kinds of odors and use disinfectants and other chemicals. We don't know how the art will react to such an environment."

"You let smokers borrow pieces. Remember that sculpture that was used inside a punch bowl," said Anne.

"The curatorial staff did not put the sculpture in the punch bowl," said Jerry. "The lack of a smoking policy is a fair point."

"Mr. Barnes is our biggest donor and pays the cleaning costs for any object he borrows," said Agatha.

"Yes, that is our acknowledged hypocrisy," said Jerry. "I think we are all in agreement about pursuing this opportunity and working out the details with the art therapist and the hospital."

"Yes," said Agatha and Anne.

"Then I would like you two to prepare an implementation plan. Anne: set up a meeting for you and Agatha with the hospital people to understand goals and expectations. Agatha: find out if there are any issues about exposing the objects to the hospital environment. If we're okay with the exposure, then work on a list of objects for use in conjunction with the potential hospital programs. Then we'll remove those objects from the lending library."

"We could lose lending fees," said Agatha.

"The hospital program is a higher priority," said Jerry. "We have to put our best foot forward. Let's meet again in two weeks for an update."

As Agatha and Anne worked on their to-do lists, they answered the following questions:

1. Which curatorial and program materials can be used off-site? What other interpretive tools could be used off-site that might not be used on-site?
2. How should the museum staff balance the intellectual integrity of its interpretive and educational materials with the needs of the art therapist?
3. What protocols should implemented for managing the deaccessioned collection for off-site programs?

Other questions to consider:

1. What are the advantages and disadvantages of a museum developing a slate of offsite-only programs and then finding off-site partners? Should the museum first identify off-site partners and then develop the programs?
2. What are the roles and responsibilities of the program, education, and curatorial staff in off-site programs?
3. How can museum/history associations, like AASLH or AAM, facilitate partnerships between museums and other organizations?

CASE 3: CARON CARTOGRAPHIC SOCIETY

The Caron Cartographic Society is housed in a Federalist-style mansion in a historic residential neighborhood. Local real estate developer, Ted Graziano, has tried to redevelop the neighborhood for a decade. Instead of tearing down the historic homes, Graziano has a new plan: registering the neighborhood as a National Historic District. Graziano tries to persuade Caron Board Chair Richard Sherman and Museum Director Michelle Shennan to support his plans.

Museum Background

Late-nineteenth-century explorer Elwood Caron enjoyed cold climates. The heat and humidity of his hometown of Athens drove him to Alaska and the Arctic. After a lifetime of Arctic exploration and map-making, Caron returned to his hometown and assembled a noteworthy collection of Arctic maps and exploration journals, which he shared with fellow Arctic explorers and enthusiasts.

Since scholars already came to Caron's house to view his collection, his family decided to turn his house into a museum/archive after his death in 1918.

The Caron Cartographic Society enjoyed a robust membership whose annual dues and donations provided the majority of the one hundred and fifty thousand dollar annual budget. Loan and reproduction fees also contributed. While actual museum attendance averaged a seemingly small one thousand people per year, the town regarded the Caron as its premier scholarly institution. A seat on the Caron board was prized.

Richard Sherman, the current board chair, was Elwood's grandson and the president of the local bank. In his banker's role, he met frequently with Ted Graziano, a local real estate developer. The two men had known each other for fifty years and could usually predict the other's reaction to proposals. Richard was surprised when Ted asked to meet with Richard and Michelle Shennan, the Caron's director.

Ted's Pitch

Michelle and Richard agreed to meet Ted at the Caron. Ted did not disclose why he wanted to speak with them.

"I think he bought all the surrounding properties and is going to build a shopping center around us," said Michelle.

"His dream is to build a huge subdivision and name it after himself," said Richard. "I checked, and none of our neighbors have sold recently. He still owns the three properties across the street."

"Yes, I do," said Ted. "The door was unlocked, so I came right in. I figured you would be excited to see me."

"Curious is the right word," said Richard.

"You're a stickler for accuracy, Richard," said Ted. "Accuracy is the key to my plan. Profitability, too. Accuracy and profitability—the keys to a banker's heart. I'm not forgetting you, Michelle. My plan is also very historic."

"Thank you," said Michelle. "My curiosity is overwhelming. What's this accurate, historical, profitable plan?"

"So, you know the town council has blocked my plan for the Grazianovillas. Not in synch with the neighborhood. Too futuristic. This is the twenty-first century. Get on board. Then, I realized, the future is the past, like Celebration in Florida or those old house rehab shows on TV. You can't fight city hall, so I'm going all in on the past."

"What does that mean?" asked Richard.

"Historic district!" said Ted.

"Historic district?" asked Richard.

"Yes! I'm going to have this area declared an historic district and go all in on the charm," said Ted.

"The tax credits are a nice bonus," said Michelle. "You can't just declare a national historic district. You have to research to find out if the area meets the criteria and then write up the nomination. The state committee reviews the nomination and makes it recommendation to the National Registrar."

"See, I knew you would know all about it," said Ted. "I figured you would want to write the nomination."

"I've never written a nomination. I've read them. You have to make the historical argument for inclusion. You're basically writing a research paper and filling out a long government form. If you're serious, you should hire a consulting firm that specializes in nominations."

"Do you know any?"

"No."

"I can figure that out. I've read the Schmickle, so I have the game plan. The details will work themselves out. I really need a statement of support from the Caron."

"Why?" asked Richard.

"You'll be affected by the designation. As a historic building and a museum, people take you seriously; gives the movement more credibility if you're on board."

"This is a lot to think about," said Richard.

"When can I schedule a press conference to announce your support?"

"I don't know," said Richard. "We have a lot to think about."

"You're so cautious, Richard. I figured you'd need time to add and subtract. No problem. I have other ducks to line up. The Schmickle said it was hard work dealing with all the stakeholders."

"We appreciate that you came to us before any public announcement," said Michelle. "The entire board has to discuss your proposal and decide our position."

"No problem. I'll call you at the end of the week for an update." With that, Ted left the building. Michelle and Richard sat in silence for a few minutes.

Reviewing Ted's Pitch

"What is a Schmickle?" asked Richard.

"He's a person. Schmickle wrote a book about activism in historical preservation. How to rally the community and government to support historic preservation projects," said Michelle. "As I recall, it was a very good, practical guide to local politics."

"If Ted pulls off this historic designation, what are the consequences to us?"

"We are eligible for tax credits if we rehab the building. They will put up special street signs. We could use it for marketing purposes, but attendance isn't critical for us."

"We can still manage the museum and the building per board direction. We don't need special permits or government approvals for our plans or budgets?"

"Correct. If any federal building projects are planned for the area, they have to assess the impact on the historic district as a whole. There's no real impact on our daily operations. The designation is more about prestige and development tax credits, which is why Ted is now in the history business."

"So there is no practical downside to supporting the designation?"

"Just agreeing with Ted."

"Exactly. He is putting us in an awkward position. We normally avoid commenting on political or real estate issues, but he is ensnaring us in his latest scheme. We have to say something."

"The state board may take a dim view of a real estate developer pushing for a historical designation to fatten his own wallet. I don't necessarily think the designation is a bad thing. It could help some of our neighbors who have wanted to repair their homes but are struggling with the cost."

"The rest of the board will not be enthused about supporting Ted in any way. We definitely will not participate in any press conferences."

"What if we say we support the concept of a historical district and look forward to the state board's review of the nomination?"

"I think we should only comment if directly asked. We don't need to volunteer information."

"We're going to be asked. Staff and board need to have responses. Once we respond and reiterate that same response, the press should tire of asking. Since we aren't speaking against the nomination, Ted should leave us alone, too."

"He will push for an explicit statement of support."

"But he knows we won't make one."

Richard and Michelle decided to call a board meeting to discuss a position statement about Ted's plan. They knew the board would have to answer the following questions:

1. How does the proposal affect the museum?
2. Why is the board publicly responding to the proposal?
3. What issues should be addressed in the board's response?

Other questions to consider:

1. How can Richard separate his personal feelings about Ted from his evaluation of the merits of Ted's proposal?
2. What is a museum's responsibility to its neighbors?
3. If the board decides to support the nomination, how should the museum participate in the process?

EPILOGUE

Community engagement takes many forms. A museum can bring its knowledge off-site or be brought into political debates because of its position as a trusted public institution. The questions at the core of these case studies are: Does a museum have a special obligation to formulate a position on relevant issues? Does the obligation end by communicating that position? Is a museum also obliged to advocate for its position?

Both the Owens Veteran's Museum and the Caron Cartographic Society are respected members of their communities, who are expected to respond to these local political issues that directly affect them. The Corbett Art Museum's history of community disengagement is now impairing its viability; it seeks to reestablish its public trust. As you craft your responses to the questions, consider the roles of museums in public life and the repercussions of both vocal activism and mute passivity.

Chapter 8

Marketing

INTRODUCTION

Like for-profit businesses, museums and historic sites have products and services to sell. They also have to introduce, establish, and reinforce their institutional identity with the public. Marketing is the process of promoting those goods, services, and identities to people. The relationship between customers/guests/visitors and a museum or historic site is deeper than a simple commercial transaction or brand loyalty. Mission fulfillment depends on the ability of museums and historic sites to introduce themselves to the public and then to convince the public to share their missions. Institutions should consider marketing as that process of introduction and continuous invitations to participate in institutional events and mission support activities. Though an institution may not have a specific staff member assigned to market the institution, every staff member can be an ambassador for his/her institution.

This chapter features three case studies exploring:

- institutional reputation;
- staff skills;
- marketing messages; and
- the use of technology.

Budget establishes parameters for marketing campaigns, but technology has enabled new, lower cost ways to connect with people. A large marketing budget cannot increase people's connections with an institution that cannot effectively define or communicate its mission. As you develop solutions to the questions asked at the end of each case study, consider how and what your institution communicates to the public.

CASE 1: ABRAHAM MUSIC BOX MUSEUM

Years of declining attendance and donations have forced the board of the Abraham Music Box Museum to implement a three-year turnaround plan. Frustrated by lack of substantial progress in one year, the board considers closing the museum. Museum Director Vivian Williams persuades the board to keep the museum open to complete the turnaround plan. The board agrees, if Vivian can reduce the museum's budget by 20 percent. Membership and Marketing Manager Rose Washington proposes eliminating all paper collateral, which will satisfy the budget reduction goal. The other staff is unsure about moving completely to electronic communication.

Museum Background

Bea Abraham, the wife of a local industrialist, loved music. She commissioned music boxes to play her favorite works. The quality and craftsmanship of the boxes were highly regarded. When Bea hosted fundraisers for the local symphony, the music boxes were played. The most generous donor received a box as a thank you gift.

Bea's intent was to leave the music boxes to the symphony for use as fundraising gifts. Upon her death in 1973, the symphony received the boxes. By 1975, the symphony decided to use other gifts for fundraising and sought another use for the music boxes. Several art museums and the local historical society declined the collection. Then Bea's friends decided that the collection should have its own museum and founded the Abraham Music Box Museum in 1977.

Expectations for the museum were modest. The first board rented a small storefront in a Victorian house; its fellow tenants were a tearoom and a yarn shop. The museum staff was all volunteers. The museum was open three days per week. The townspeople of Brooksville were all surprised when the museum celebrated its thirtieth anniversary.

Donations from Bea's friends had sustained the museum for its first thirty years. A twenty-first-century existence demanded new supporters and a new vision for the museum. Museum Director Vivian Williams began her tenure in 2009 and believed that the collection was a foundation for education about music, craftsmanship, and the passion of a collector. Bea's music boxes were also noteworthy in Brooksville's local history. Vivian recruited her friends Rose Washington and Stella Morgan, as membership and marketing manager and programs and curatorial manager, respectively. The three women reached out to music societies, colleges and universities, and other museums to promote the collection.

As the collection began to attract scholarly interest, the board told Vivian that it wanted to close the museum. She persuaded them to instead approve her three-year turnaround plan. If the plan failed to meet its targets, the museum could close. Vivian knew that the board would probably close the museum regardless. Her goal was to increase awareness and interest in the collection, which could inspire another institution to acquire the collection.

The Board Meeting

Vivian arrived at the board meeting, pleased about the three scholarly articles that used the collection and about the loan of several boxes to a national museum's exhibition. She presented copies of the articles and the exhibition catalog.

"We are almost half-way through our turnaround plan and are on-target with our goals," said Vivian. "We cohosted four events with the tearoom last year and already have four booked this year. We saw a 15 percent increase in revenue due to those programs."

"You and the girls are doing a good job," said Phil Zullo, the board chair and a friend of Bea's husband. "This thing is never going to make money."

"It can't generate enough revenue solely from program attendance and loan fees to fund the budget. Every museum needs donations to bridge the gap between expenses and income," said Vivian.

"This isn't a real museum," said Kimberly Wheeler, the daughter of one of Bea's friends who inherited her mother's board seat. "No one cares about music boxes any more. The board members are the only people donating. It's just silly."

"We told you to resign," said Phil. "We can manage without you."

"Bea was my mother's best friend," said Kimberly. "I have more right to be here than anyone else. Bea never wanted a museum. We should have donated the boxes years ago."

"No one wanted them," said Phil. "The only other option was to sell them and give the money to the symphony. Your mom led the opposition to that idea. Do you want to do that now?"

"It would be a better use of them," said Kimberly.

"Slow down," said Alex Gunderson, board member and Abraham family attorney. "The board has already approved a three-year turnaround plan that is meeting its goals. All of us agreed to give Vivian and the staff three years. We knew what our individual contributions would be. Are you reneging on your promise?"

"Yes," said Kimberly. "I'm not throwing good money after bad."

"I don't want to renege. We are making money and getting some publicity," said Phil.

"I'm comfortable maintaining my commitment," said Alex.

"It doesn't matter," said Kimberly. "They don't have enough money to go on for another year and a half."

"What if we come up with a plan to continue for the remainder of the turn-around time without additional board contributions?" asked Vivian.

"You would have to cut about 20 percent of the budget," said Alex.

"If we can do it," said Vivian, "will you let us complete our plan?"

"Sure," said Kimberly. Phil and Alex agreed.

After reviewing a few more items, the meeting adjourned. Vivian wasn't sure what she would say to Stella and Rose, but she was happy about the reprieve and sad about Kimberly's comments.

The Museum Staff Meets

Vivian recounted the board meeting to Stella and Rose. After she finished, they all collected their thoughts.

"I'm sorry about proposing the budget cut. I just want that extra year and a half for the collection," said Vivian.

"We would have done the same thing," said Stella. "This poor collection— it's had quite a life and deserves to be appreciated. At least we are making progress with other institutions."

"Ladies," said Rose, "are we prepared to be radical?"

"What do you mean?" asked Vivian.

"I know how to cut 20 percent of our budget and increase awareness of the collection," said Rose.

"How?" asked Vivian and Stella.

"Go paperless," said Rose. "Our biggest costs are the quarterly member magazine and monthly program schedules. We already have the e-newsletter and can still print a few posters and postcards for our programs. We only need five to ten posters, which we can print at the copy shop. Ordering one hundred postcards is pretty cheap. Everything else should be electronic. Then people can forward to their friends."

"I thought the member survey opposed an e-magazine," said Vivian.

"We have e-mail addresses for 85 percent of the members," said Rose. "We have shared our postage and paper costs with them. We need to just pull the trigger."

"I'm surprised that you want to risk alienating members," said Stella.

"The membership fee has been $10 per year for over a decade because the board won't approve an increase," said Rose. "Between the annual member party and the publications, we lose about $20 per member. Honestly, few actually visit the museum or attend programs. Most renew in memory of Bea rather than any interest in the museum. Realistically, we are marketing this collection to other institutions, desperately hoping someone will want it. That was the secret goal of the turnaround plan."

"Yes, but we were also hoping that the community would see the outside appreciation of the collection and save the museum," said Vivian. "Let's take this step-by-step and focus on our immediate goals. The board does like the glossy member magazine and has balked at previous attempts to change it."

"Then Kimberly can restore her contribution," said Rose.

"Well, we could say that we are participating in the town's Go Green initiative," said Stella.

"Yes," said Rose, "the environment reporter at the paper is looking for a big money example. We would be saving a few thousand dollars and could get a nice feature article."

"The board would be more amenable to participating in Go Green than just cutting the glossy," said Vivian. "What about the program schedule? How will people know about the programs?"

"We already duplicate that information in the paper postcards and our e-newsletter," said Rose. "The paper monthly program schedule was created for that board member who liked to post a calendar on her fridge. The only people who get the paper version are museum visitors. We have more people on our e-mail list than visitors. Our e-newsletter provider allows us to send more communications than we currently do, so no cost increase there."

"We do have so many beautiful digital images," said Stella. "People will want to forward the e-mails to their friends. More people will learn about us."

"Exactly," said Rose. "What else can we cut? The rest of the budget is spent on rent and collection maintenance."

"We could be a virtual museum," said Stella. "Paying for storage is cheaper than paying rent. We could still run programs with the tea room."

"I thought I was the radical one," said Rose.

"Let's not get too radical," said Vivian. "The board seems to be looking for a way out. I don't want to give them too many ideas. I still think the museum is important to our town's history and to preserve the work of all those anonymous craftsmen. We should focus on finding partners who can help us with those goals."

"So if we go paperless, we meet the budget cut order, we will probably get a news feature about going green, and might increase awareness of the collection," said Rose. "I vote yes."

"I agree," said Stella.

"I agree," said Vivian. "Now I have to persuade the board."

"I can create sample electronic versions of the member magazine and program schedule," said Rose. "Seeing a sample helps. I can also contact the newspaper and see if the reporter bites."

"Thank you," said Vivian. "We need all the help we can get."

As the staff prepared materials for the board, they knew they must answer the following questions:

1. How will the museum prepare members for the switch to an electronic member magazine?
2. What are the differences between the budget line items for electronic and print publications? Consider factors like staff time, e-vendor subscriptions, and list maintenance. Is the electronic version cheaper than the print version?
3. How can the museum staff quantify the potential new audience that could be reached by electronic communications?

Other questions to consider:

1. Is the museum staff relying too much on marketing to save the museum? Why or why not?
2. Should a museum director use marketing techniques to persuade the board to implement preferred policies? Why or why not?
3. If a museum is in danger of closing, should it publicize its situation? Why or why not?

CASE 2: MOORE THEATRE MUSEUM

A producer from the cable show *Paranormal Pursuits* calls Phoebe Preston, the program and marketing manager of the Moore Theatre Museum, about shooting a segment at the museum. The focus of the piece is the suicide of an actress on-site when the museum was still a working theater. The museum has tried to distance itself from that event, though it does offer Halloween ghost tours. The museum is concerned about promoting itself as a site of tragedy, instead of a site of theater studies, to a national audience.

Museum Background

The Moore Theatre had been a key stop on the secondary theater and vaudeville circuits of the late nineteenth and early twentieth century. As other theaters in town turned into movie theaters or the homes of local theatrical troupes, the Moore struggled to find its place. In 1942, a committee was formed to determine the fate of the Moore after it had been foreclosed upon. Since the citizens of Yorkville were avid theatergoers and also participated in local theater companies, the committee decided to turn the Moore into a theater museum. In the subsequent decades, the Moore Theatre Museum was a beloved and successful local institution, dedicated to educating and inspiring the community through the history and art of theater.

Each generation and each museum director had to decide how to interpret the most significant event in the building's history: the 1923 suicide of actress Jeanne Morgan, who killed herself after being replaced as Ophelia in a production of Hamlet. The tragic irony further sensationalized the story. Initially, the Moore ignored the event, refusing to acknowledge its occurrence. As time passed and the Moore's exhibitions and programs won national awards, the museum staff slowly began to incorporate the story into interpretation and developed an annual Halloween ghost story that mentioned the story. The Moore contextualized the event and did not use Jeanne Morgan's name in promotional materials.

The Phone Call

Phoebe Preston, the programs and marketing manager, and Irene Kline, the events manager, shared an office. After returning from showing the space to potential customers, Irene was surprised to hear Phoebe speaking animatedly on the telephone.

"That would be very difficult," said Phoebe. "We normally don't focus on that. . . . Yes, I understand, but we really aren't prepared or equipped. . . . That turnaround time is very tight. The director has to approve, and we might need board approval. Yes, I will present the offer. I'm being honest with you. . . . You can certainly do that, but that isn't very compelling. . . . I'll call you back tomorrow. Good-bye."

"Someone trying to sell you a full page remnant ad in a gossip magazine?" asked Irene.

"I wish," said Phoebe. "That's an automatic no. Have you ever heard of *Paranormal Pursuits*?"

"Is it some type of video game?"

"No, it's a TV show."

"One of those ghost hunting shows?"

"Exactly, they want to shoot a segment about Jeanne, including a reenactment."

"That sounds tacky. Wait, I found an episode on the web."

After watching a couple of episodes, Phoebe and Irene agreed that the production values were good, and the reenactments were melodramatic. Phoebe then called Museum Director Kevin Drew, who joined the women in their office and viewed the episodes.

The Staff Discussion

Phoebe recounted the details of her phone conversation with the *Paranormal Pursuits* producers.

"They need two days and one night to shoot the interviews and reenactment. Either John (the Moore's curator) or I could do the interviews," said Phoebe. "If we don't let them use the theater, they will take some street shots and use another theater for the reenactment. The schedule is pretty rigid. They set up the ghost busting equipment on day one and shoot the reenactment, which activates the spirits. Then the spirits come out at night while their team is hovered over the ghost busting equipment. The staff interviews are done on day two."

"One of the staff would have to stay with them overnight," said Kevin.

"I can do it," said Irene. "I'm used to be being here at night and know all the shadows. I have no problem keeping the production crew in line."

"They are willing to pay," said Phoebe. "So we could bill it as a facility rental."

"Then I'm definitely in favor," said Irene.

"Hold on," said Kevin. "There are other considerations. I really don't like their heavy-handed approach. A friend of mine at a science museum was interviewed by one of those cheesy museum reality shows. They wanted her to refer to people with acromegaly as freaks and to display pictures of medical deformities—very sensationalistic and inconsistent with the museum's mission."

"Yes, I've seen that show," said Phoebe. "Some of the segments are well-done. I am bothered when the museum participates too enthusiastically with the concept. The educational content should be the priority; too bad if it's not compelling television."

"I thought your job was to share the museum with the world," teased Irene.

"Yes, a museum, not a sideshow," said Phoebe.

"The problem is our hypocrisy," said Kevin. "I assume they learned about Jeanne from our ghost tour."

"The sister of one of their producers went on the tour and told her brother," said Phoebe. "So we created the situation."

"It's not that bad," said Irene. "She took poison, which isn't too gruesome. A few hundred thousand people will see the show. Even if they don't visit, they could buy something on the website."

"Do we have any control over the content?" asked Kevin.

"They need our help with the voice-overs and reenactment script. You saw the Pursuers. Classic faux scientist-adventurers," said Phoebe. "It was a tragic, rather than a scandalous, event. By all accounts, she thought Ophelia was her last chance at stardom and was devastated at being fired. What do you think the board will say?"

"We actually discussed a similar scenario when we worked on the strategic plan," said Kevin. "We had to talk about sacred cows and decision-making responsibilities. The board decided that museum staff were better qualified to evaluate such situations. The board was willing to publicly engage with this story. I was surprised because Jeanne's second cousin is on the board."

"Really? Who?" asked Irene.

"We can't say," said Kevin. "If you dig around in public records and trace the family tree, you can figure it out. The person keeps it quiet because some family members are still upset about the ghost tours."

"How will they react to the TV show?" said Phoebe. "If we do it, we'll have to talk about it on our website and newsletters."

"From what you've said, the show is going to happen no matter what we do," said Kevin. "If we choose to participate, we have some leverage. From a museum reputation point of view, we would be just one of many museums who have participated in these types of shows. Within our peers, I am comfortable that we are respected. What do you think Phoebe?"

"I'd rather be profiled in a national magazine or on PBS, but I don't think we will be embarrassed or harmed by the show," said Phoebe.

"I think we should charge them three times our normal facility rental fee," said Irene.

"You can handle that negotiation," said Kevin. "I have complete faith in you."

"So we're doing it?" asked Irene.

Kevin said that the three of them first had to draft answers to anticipated questions to justify participation in the show. Those questions were:

1. How will the museum benefit from appearing on the TV show?
2. What are the potential risks of appearing on the TV show?
3. What role should the participation fee play in the decision?

Other questions to consider:

1. How can a museum balance interpretive integrity and reputational risk when dealing with the media?
2. If the museum refuses to cooperate with the show, how should it publicly respond when the episode airs?
3. What issues or situations should be addressed in a museum's media policy?

CASE 3: HARRISON MINIATURE HOUSE MUSEUM

The Harrison Miniature House Museum is preparing for the opening of a new exhibition. Intern Jackie Coolidge has volunteered to create an app for the new exhibition. Curator Grace Adams and Marketing Coordinator Julia Madison like the idea. Museum Director Martha Tyler is hesitant because of the precedent and maintenance issues. All agree that the museum should integrate more social media and technology tools, but disagree on the how and the what.

Museum Background

The story of the Harrison Miniature House Museum, founded in 1965, surprised most visitors. Grover Harrison was a mechanical engineer and frustrated architect. His talent was building miniature versions of buildings, rather than drafting original plans. He worked as a mechanical engineer at a local tool and die factory and built small-scale replicas of famous and representative houses as a hobby. Museums would hire Grover to build miniatures for them. His skill was well-known.

When Grover retired, he decided to start his own museum. People enjoyed seeing his work, and he was tired of them ringing his doorbell at all hours. A museum had regular hours. Grover also taught people how to create miniatures. Parents discovered that their children were excited to learn math and physics from Grover. Architecture and engineering students at the local university preferred Grover's classes and improved in their college studies afterward.

By the early 1970s, the Harrison Miniature House Museum was well-established, with strong academic and community ties—able to continue after Grover's death in 1975. Math, physics, and engineering professionals sat on the board and staffed the education department. Retired professionals were the backbone of the volunteer corps. The Harrison prided itself on staying current with technology. It had one of the first museum websites in the region. The rapid development in social media technology challenged even the Harrison. The staff embraced technology, but was concerned about the accelerated pace of obsolescence. A new technology appeared for almost every exhibition. Though the Harrison was typically a leader in adoption, Museum Director Martha Tyler was increasingly concerned about the ever-increasing staff, data, and equipment costs. She scrutinized any new tool or technology requests.

The New Exhibition

Curator Grace Adams and Marketing Coordinator Julia Madison met to discuss the marketing campaign for the upcoming exhibition *The Detail of*

Scale: Reproducing Furniture. In addition to the exhibition website, print collateral, and ads, the team was considering an app. Jackie Coolidge, a curatorial intern, said that she knew how to program apps. The project would also be an important piece of her graduation portfolio. Grace and Julia thought it was a win–win situation and asked Jackie to prepare a presentation.

"I'm curious to see what she has," said Julia.

"She's been working on a prototype," said Grace. "She interviewed some of the craftsmen and was reviewing all the photographs. Jackie is very talented. I hope Martha appreciates the effort."

"Martha appreciates good work," said Julia. "She worries about cost. Even if we don't use the app, Jackie will still have it for her portfolio."

"A live project is better than a prototype," said Grace.

"Am I interrupting?" asked Jackie.

"No, please come in," said Julia. "Grace has been telling me about your work. I'm very excited to see it."

"Oh, well," said Jackie, "we'll see if it's any good after you see it."

"You should always be confident in your work when giving a presentation," said Grace. "The audience will feel your confidence and be more enthused about your proposal. If you downplay your work, others will, too."

"I'm nervous," said Jackie. "I've never done a work presentation."

"I still get nervous presenting to Martha and the board," said Julia. "You'll figure out what your normal level of nerves are and forge ahead. Like Grace said, be positive about your work. The nerves will take care themselves."

"Ok," said Jackie. "I am pleased to demonstrate an app prototype for *The Detail of Scale: Reproducing Furniture* exhibition. I brought an iPhone and an iPad with the prototype, so you can see how it works on both devices."

"Excellent," said Grace.

"The app builds on the website and goes deeper into the interpretation," said Jackie. "You can view a gallery of the tools and see videos of the tools being used. It also has a pictorial dictionary of different pieces of furniture and furniture styles. You can look up Queen Anne or sideboard or Queen Anne sideboard to learn which pieces are appropriate for a room or an era. Short biographies of key designers are included. I also made a game. You see two pictures and have to guess which picture is of the full-size piece or the miniature version."

"I love that," said Julia. "Alright, Grace, let's play. Go!"

Grace and Julia played the game, and Julia won. The ladies decided that Grace was overthinking her analysis.

"I am very pleased with all the scholarship and educational materials that you have incorporated," said Grace. "Exhibition labels are always tricky for us. A tool like this helps the guests learn more and answers so many questions."

"I know Martha worries about cost," said Jackie. "We could actually charge a few dollars for the app, so it could pay for itself. It's like the next generation of audio tours."

"That's a good point," said Julia. "We don't have audio tours because the numbers didn't work. This content can also be used in promotional or educational materials beyond this exhibition."

"Exactly," said Grace. "Jackie digitized our designer bios for use in this app. We can cut and paste that information into other materials."

"I'm glad you like it," said Jackie. "Do you think Martha will like it?"

"Your presentation was very thorough and addressed cost and usage issues," said Grace. "Both Julia and I have a few suggestions to make it more Martha friendly. I think you are ready for tomorrow's presentation."

"Whew," said Jackie.

Grace and Julia helped Jackie refine her presentation for the following day's presentation to Martha. They cautioned Jackie that Martha would ask a lot of questions. The number of questions or Martha's tone of voice did not indicate Martha's approval or disapproval of a proposal. Martha was thorough and wanted to be completely certain about the pros and cons of any project.

The Martha Meeting

Jackie, Grace, and Julia entered Martha's office the following day. Jackie presented the features and functionality of the app and explained the integration of preexisting and new content. She explained how the app could be sold. Grace and Julia explained how the app could be used to support other curatorial and marketing goals.

"This is a good piece of work, Jackie," said Martha. "You expanded upon the information in the exhibition—anticipating guest questions. The visuals are consistent with our branding. The general format is flexible, so it can be used for other exhibitions or programs."

"Thank you," said Jackie.

"Your presentation style was engaging and confident," said Martha. "I do have a few questions."

"I'm ready," said Jackie.

"Is the app strictly iOS or can it be adapted for Android?"

"I only code iOS, so someone else would have to code an Android version."

"Ok. Have you ever submitted an app to the app store?"

"No. My roommate has, so she could help with that process."

"Ok. That's good to know. Have you made a revenue projection?"

"Grace and I decided not to project revenue at this point," said Julia. "We don't have a real comparator, so the three of us need to create a revenue projection formula."

"That makes sense," said Martha. "Jackie, thank you for such excellent work. Whether or not we actually roll out the app is a business decision. Your design and content maintain our high quality standards. As Grace and Julia can tell you, we have stopped other similarly well-done prototypes because of cost or logistics issues. I encourage you to include this app in your portfolio, and I am happy to write a recommendation letter for you."

"Thank you, Martha," said Jackie. "I understand completely and appreciate the opportunity to build the prototype."

After a few more minutes of conversation, Jackie left Martha's office. Martha, Grace, and Julia began discussing the feasibility of the app launch.

"Even if we don't launch the app," said Grace, "Jackie digitized a lot of our paper-only copy. We can now use that content in so many other platforms."

"The game is brilliant," said Julia. "We can use that set up for TV spots or member nights."

"The quality of the work is outstanding," said Martha. "We have a budget for a part-time curatorial assistant beginning in September. If Grace agrees, we should encourage Jackie to apply."

"Absolutely," said Grace.

"What are your concerns?" asked Julia.

"I don't think selling the app is viable," said Martha. "We would need an Android version. My brother-in-law works with apps and has said that dealing with the app stores is a pain. Then we have to maintain it and keep up with OS changes. We'd need a grant to finance those activities. The small amount of revenue would never offset those costs."

"But having an app in the app stores does expand our visibility with a younger and non-local audience," said Julia.

"We do well on Trip Advisor," said Martha. "I'd rather spend money advertising to tour operators or working with the state tourism board. We've actually seen positive returns on that spending."

"What about in-house use?" asked Grace.

"How do you mean?" asked Martha.

"We do receive requests for audio tours. We can incorporate audio into the app," said Grace. "We could write a grant to purchase a certain number of iPads, even refurbished ones would work. Then we load exhibition and general museum apps on the iPads. We can disable Internet access and control updates."

"That's still a lot of expensive equipment that could be stolen," said Martha.

"The library only lends equipment to people with driver's licenses. They take the license and a credit card number in case of damage. Your license is returned when you return the equipment, and it passes inspection," said Julia.

"What kind of inspection?" asked Grace.

"Teenage boys like to type obscenities in Notes. People take pictures. The library has a checklist. It takes about thirty seconds to check," said Julia.

"That's good to know," said Martha. "I'm still not convinced that an app is viable."

"Jackie and I can do some research on in-house apps. Utilizing technology is part of our reputation. We have been dancing around the app issue for a couple of years. If we conduct this research, we can show our due diligence," said Grace.

"If people understand the equipment and maintenance costs, we might receive donations," said Julia.

"That's good point. We need to assume that we will have to pay the initial and ongoing costs. Show me a budget with revenue sources. More importantly, convince me that an app is needed to appeal to our younger visitors. I don't think an app is necessary. We still have QR codes littering our signage. Those have to be replaced. A mobile optimized website accomplishes the same functions at a lower cost and with easier maintenance. I am willing to be wrong, but you need to convince me about the audience," said Martha.

Grace and Julia decided to work together, with Jackie, to research and then present their findings to Martha. That presentation would have to answer the following questions:

1. How is the app audience different form the website audience?
2. How will an app encourage visitation?
3. What is the difference between using an app or a website to market an exhibition versus to market the museum in general?

Other questions to consider:

1. What are the advantages/disadvantages of an audio guide versus an app?
2. How should a museum utilize the special skills or talents of an intern?
3. Should museums be early adopters or late adopters of technology for marketing purposes?

EPILOGUE

The reasons for a person's first visit to a museum vary: a friend's recommendation, guidebook's review, a serendipitous web search, or curiosity upon seeing the building. Marketing provides a way to help people find that reason. Marketing plans help you think about the different reasons why a teenager, musician, engineer, or a gardening club or a senior group might want to visit your site. The institutions in these three case studies are all searching for methods to connect with different audiences and then instigate specific actions.

The Abraham Music Box Museum may be coming to the end of its existence, but its collection may prove valuable to another institution. The Moore Theatre Museum has an opportunity to reach a national audience, but in a sensationalistic rather than educational way. The Harrison Miniature House Museum could implement a new tool to attract a younger audience, but must consider all the costs. As you think about these different scenarios and answer the questions, consider the concept of marketing as an invitation. Different technologies can always be used to deliver that invitation. You still need to create a compelling message for that invitation.

Chapter 9

Technology

INTRODUCTION

Desktop software, the Internet, and social media are just a few of the technological advances from the past forty years that enable museums to educate and inspire a limitless audience. Those boundless opportunities created by technology also require well-defined goals and objectives, staff training, and ever-changing equipment to maximize those opportunities. Technology is a tool that requires a special strategy to avoid a budgetary black hole or the selection of the wrong tool for the wrong job. Constant upgrades, changed or buried functions, bugs, and overly complex software have vexed museum professionals.

This chapter features three case studies exploring:

- the definition of audience;
- the difference between physical and digital collections;
- the technology life cycle; and
- the complexities of technology projects.

Every institution has different needs and uses for technology, but all must define the parameters for incorporating technology into their workflows. One of the cases asks you to consider creating a technology maintenance plan. As you develop solutions to the questions asked at the end of each case study, consider how the existence of such a plan would have affected the events as they unfolded. Would your own institution benefit from such plan?

CASE 1: PIKE SUFFRAGE MUSEUM

Attendance at the Pike Suffrage Museum has declined 25 percent over the past decade. Online visitation and distance learning class attendees are increasing at an average rate of 7 percent per year. Revenue is also increasing. When Board Member Cindy Terrell offhandedly remarks that the Pike should become a virtual museum, Museum Director Diana Wilson and her staff consider the possibilities in implementing that idea.

Museum Background

Suffragette Dorothy Pike organized travel tours to promote a woman's right to vote in the early twentieth century. Pike was considered scandalous because she drove her own car cross-state to promote suffrage. She was also known to wear bloomers and to smoke. After Pike's death in a plane crash in 1938, the Woman's Club of Rochester, Pike's hometown, decided to create a museum to memorialize her contribution to the suffrage movement. Because Pike was still considered a shocking personality, the museum founders decided that the museum's mission should be to educate voters and to promote voting rights, using Dorothy Pike's story as a catalyst. As time passed, the museum's mission proved effective during the 1960s civil rights movement and the 1970s women's rights movement.

   The Pike became a civic gathering place for political candidate debates, naturalization ceremonies, and voter education forums. As the Internet grew and in-person attendance fell, the Pike began experimenting with online forums and classes. People from across the country attended the online classes and even became museum members. A partnership with the local public access television station enabled live streaming of candidate debates via the Pike's website. To the surprise of the staff and the board, the Pike earned more revenue through its online programs than its in-house admissions and program fees—giving the museum greater financial stability than it had had in years.

   As Museum Director Diana Wilson began her sixth year as director, she wondered how sustainable the online success would be. She also wished more people would come to the museum to see Dorothy Pike's car and the Ballot Box exhibition. School groups still came, but regular visitors appeared less frequently.

The Board Lunch

Each month, Diana had informal lunches with board members. These casual gatherings helped new board members form relationships with existing board members and gave Diana an opportunity to chat with board members about the museum industry and local news. Board Member Cindy Terrell had missed a few lunches, so she and Diana scheduled a separate lunch.

"I'm glad we finally have a chance to catch up," said Diana.

"My work traveling schedule has been crazy," said Cindy. "One of my coworkers had the flu, so I took his place at a bunch of meetings. I'm sorry for missing our lunches."

"It happens. The winter was really quiet. The big board excitement was Marvin's new hot toddy recipe. At the museum, we've been working on the next round of grant applications. Non-election years are a nice breather."

"Well, there is something I wanted to ask you about."

"Okay."

"I've been looking at the attendance figures. Technically, overall attendance has been around forty thousand per year for the past fifteen years. The percent of in-house visitors has gone from 95 percent to 40 percent."

"Yes, the numbers are fascinating. Over the same period of time, our expenses have increased by 15 percent, and our revenue by 45 percent."

"Exactly. The in-person attendance is primarily the school groups, naturalization ceremonies, and special forums. All those activities are scheduled. I ran the numbers. If we move to appointment only hours and focus on the digital offerings, we would decrease expenses by 20 percent."

"So switch to being a virtual and appointment only institution?"

"Yes, it's much more cost effective, and we are reaching a broader audience."

"The board has discussed the implications of this trend toward the virtual. Since we were initially founded to support local voting and elections, we still have an obligation to be physically accessible to the community."

"Sure, but we don't need to keep the lights on when no one is in the front part of the building."

"Definitely something to think about."

"We have to be realistic about people's habits. People just don't go to museums very often anymore."

"Attention for eyeballs is more competitive."

"It is. Well, I'm sure we'll be talking about this at board meetings."

As the ladies continued their lunch, Diana pondered Cindy's comments. The numbers didn't lie. Online engagement was the future, and the Pike seemed to be a leader. Diana's fellow museum directors were impressed that the Pike generated enough revenue from its online programs to cover the costs. Diana wondered if she was being a fuddy-duddy about the museum building. She decided to discuss Cindy's suggestions with Curator Mary Greene and Program and Education Coordinator Jean Ross.

The Discussion

Diana recounted her conversation with Cindy to Mary and Jean. She then shared her personal reservations about limiting access to the museum.

"I don't know if it's because I grew up pre-computers, but I see an intrinsic value in viewing the physical collection. A digital reproduction doesn't convey the heft and complexities of operating Dorothy's car, for example. People are always surprised by its size and all the gears," said Diana.

"Cindy didn't say close the museum," said Jean. "She was wondering about the viability of our Tuesday through Saturday hours. We've talked about that ourselves."

"Cindy's a numbers person," said Mary. "We asked her to join the board because of that expertise. As a curator, I want people to experience our collection in its reality. Creating online programs using our audio and video clips does allow us to share those materials with a wider audience. Selfishly, I still want people to come here and see my real exhibits."

"My fundamental question is what is our obligation to our local community," said Diana. "We were founded to support voter education and voting rights in Rochester. Over time, the 'in Rochester' part was dropped. Where does our geography begin and end now with the Internet? We have a three person staff and ten volunteers. I think we need parameters."

"I've encountered that problem with our educational materials. People from other countries download our voting rights course packs and also need materials about American national, state, and local government levels to understand the course packs," said Jean. "I do struggle with deciding what knowledge I should assume people have and what other basic history educational materials to provide. Sometimes I wonder who our audience is."

"Our Internet success is making the problem worse. It would be easier if we weren't making any money," said Diana.

"I think we should answer these questions now," said Mary. "The board will ask them. As time goes on, we will have a harder time convincing the board to maintain our building. I don't want to work in a warehouse."

"Without the collection, we don't have a museum," said Diana. "The schools enjoy their visits. One of the state requirements is working with primary sources, so our building is necessary."

"To Cindy's point, we rarely have visitors on Wednesdays, Thursdays, and Fridays," said Jean. "Tuesdays are school groups, and Saturdays are regular visitors. We could do appointment only Wednesday through Friday. We could still do group tours, but avoid those long stretches of crickets. The volunteers do get bored, even with the special projects."

"Do we want to propose that?" asked Mary.

"I don't want to solve a problem that isn't yet a problem," said Diana. "Let's think about options, answers, and repercussions. I keep coming back to our civic responsibility. I'm not sure if I want to give up on convincing people to visit the museum. After another generation, the Internet and smart devices will be normal tools. People still want to connect with one another in-person."

Diana, Mary, and Jean thought about the points Cindy raised and the questions their discussion created. They decided to formalize their thoughts about an online versus a physical museum presence. They answered the following questions:

1. What are the values of the online and physical collection and programs?
2. What role should revenue generation play in resource allocation to support or expand online or physical collections and programs?
3. If virtual visitation continues to rise and in-person visitation continues to decline, how should the museum admission hours be adjusted?

Other questions to consider:

1. Should museums adjust their mission statements to clarify their in-person and online missions?
2. How should curatorial and education departments serve the needs of online visitors?
3. How can museums convince the public of the value in viewing the physical collection?

CASE 2: GREAT PLAINS HISTORICAL SOCIETY

Great Plains Historical Society IT Director Steve Baker discovers that CD-ROMs containing photographs, whose originals were destroyed in a flood, are deteriorating. He and Curator Penny Linus realize that other digital collections are also at risk and that the costs and consequences of continuous transfer to new technologies may not be feasible. Museum Director Bill Workman tasks Steve and Penny with drafting a technology transfer plan.

Museum Background

Founded in 1911, the Great Plains Historical Society collected and preserved the history of the western half of the state. The society's founders had always maintained good relationships with the local Indian tribes, who entrusted artifacts to the Society. The tribes also allowed the Society's photographers to photograph certain ceremonies and daily routines. Those photographs formed the Great Plains Indian Photograph Collection, which was a key collection for the Society. Scholars, artists, and filmmakers used its contents. The tribes still attended any exhibitions that used the photographs and participated in museum programs. By the 2000s, fewer people were interested in the collection, though it remained a priority collection for the Society.

Many of the original negatives had been lost over the years. The prints were carefully stored and were the subject of the Society's first digitization grant in 1995. All the photos were scanned and stored on CD-ROMs. The prints were returned to storage. A terrible flood submerged most of the storage space in 2004. Some of the prints were restored; others were permanently destroyed. The CD-ROMs were spared. Every year, the IT director and the curator assessed the condition of the prints and the CD-ROMs.

The Annual Assessment

IT Director Steve Baker began the annual technical assessment every January. Attendance was at its nadir that month, so Steve and the rest of the staff schedule administrative projects for that time.

Steve first conducted a visual inspection of the items, checking for flaws, damage, or dirt. If needed, he cleaned the item. Then he played or viewed the item on the appropriate device. Last year, he and Penny Linus, the curator, had briefly discussed transferring the photographs from the CD-ROMs to hard drives or the cloud. Since budget cuts loomed and the CD-ROMs appeared okay, they decided to apply for grants to fund the transfer. They assumed that they would have two to four years before the CD-ROMs would begin to deteriorate, so they were not overly concerned when they did not receive funding in the prior year.

Steve had just completed another grant application when he decided to review the CD-ROMs. The first five looked good.

"No, no, no," said Steve.

"What's wrong?" asked Gary, an IT manager.

"Come look at the CDs," said Steve.

"Are those scratch marks?"

"I was hoping you didn't see them."

"How'd they get scratched?"

"I don't know."

Steve and Gary inserted the CD-ROMs into the computer and began to view the photos. A wavy line appeared across all the photos.

"The photos themselves look okay," said Gary. "No quality degradation at the top or bottom. It's just the wavy line through the center."

"That's still a problem," said Steve.

"I know, but a photo editor might be able to fix that."

"These are museum photos. Alterations are a problem. Maybe it's the machine. Let's try another."

Steve and Gary tried three different machines, but the wavy line remained on six CD-ROMs.

"Do you want to Google it?" asked Gary.

"It doesn't really matter. The solution will cost money. Bill and Penny have to make that decision," said Steve.

"Why would people use CD-ROMs? They're so old."

"When you were a baby, CDs were the new technology," laughed Steve. "Ten years from now, someone will ask you why you used the cloud."

"Wow, that's scary."

"My conversation with Bill and Penny will be scarier."

After Steve finished checking all the CD-ROMs, he went to Penny's office.

Steve and Penny Meet

Penny was planning several exhibitions that would use the Great Plains Indian Photograph Collection. When the technology grant applications were not accepted, Penny sought other funding possibilities. Her collections and exhibitions budgets could contribute, but the sheer number of photographs required extraordinary means. The fundraising department liked collections-based appeals and was considering a campaign for the photographs. Other projects had already been approved for the current year's campaign.

"Hey," said Steve.

"You should close the door," said Penny. "I assume you have bad news."

"Six of the CDs have wavy lines in the center of the picture."

"I know you did this, but I have to ask. Did you check them on other machines?"

"We used four machines to test them."

Penny sat silent.

"I recommend sending them to a lab that specializes in this type of recovery," said Steve. "We should probably transfer the rest, too."

"Bill is not going to be happy," said Penny. "He wanted to print them all of the CDs and maintain hard copies, but the board thought the digital solution was more cost effective."

"Compared to physical storage, it is. The pace of technological change is so fast. I recommend the cloud today, but it could be replaced tomorrow."

"At a minimum we have to fix these CDs. We don't have the negatives or prints, so these images have to be saved. The other CDs are okay, so we still have time to raise money for them. How many images are on each CD?"

"About one thousand."

"So six thousand images—that's not horrible. Development might be able to persuade some donors to fund an emergency rescue campaign."

"When do you want to tell Bill?"

"We already have a meeting scheduled for Thursday afternoon to review the assessment results. This is urgent, but not minute-by-minute time sensitive. His schedule is pretty packed this week. I can wait."

"Okay by me."

Steve and Penny decided to focus on fixing the six damaged CD-ROMs. Steve contacted some labs for cost estimates, and he and Penny checked their budgets for funds.

Steve and Penny Meet with Bill

At the regularly scheduled meeting, Steve and Penny reviewed the results of the annual IT assessment of the digital collection.

"Overall, we're in good shape, with one exception," said Steve. "Six of the Great Plains Indian CD-ROMs have a wavy line. We've look at the CDs on four machines and have the same issue. I've found some labs that think they can recover the images. They want to see the CDs before submitting a quote."

"How did that happen?" asked Bill Workman, the museum director.

"They were fine last year and stored with the rest of the hundred CDs in that collection. It may just be natural deterioration," said Steve.

"So the rest could go at any moment," said Bill.

"That's correct," said Penny. "We've been applying for grants to transfer the pictures to the cloud and to make prints. We're waiting for an acceptance."

"You want to put them in the cloud?" asked Bill. "I question the security and accessibility of the cloud. Why haven't we moved the collection to external hard drives? Then we could keep one copy on-site and another off-site."

"We could have one copy on a hard drive and one in the cloud," said Steve. The technology changes so quickly that we need flexibility. If you use proper passwords, the cloud is secure."

"Given the significance of the collection," said Penny, "I also recommend making prints. Paper has proven its stability—even with the flood."

"How much budget are we going to have to allocate to maintain and upgrade all our digital collections?" asked Bill.

"We're applying for grants," began Penny.

"Forget the grants," interrupted Bill. "We're past the point of simple digitization projects. We've moved into maintenance. Grants don't pay the electric bill. Funders like novel projects. We have to assume the costs of maintaining and upgrading our digital collections. What's our digital policy?"

"Well, we evaluate and try to replace our computers and software every five years. We stay current with upgrades," said Steve.

"No, for the digital collections. How do we determine when a collection needs to be moved to a different media?"

"We conduct our annual audit," said Penny. "If we suspect or uncover an issue, then we work on a grant application or a fundraising plan with development."

"Do you know how long CDs last?" asked Bill.

"Yes, there are lifespan estimates for CDs, DVDs, and other media," said Steve.

"So we, meaning you two, can create a maintenance plan. We have a plan for our HVAC system and other building issues. I can look at the plan and know when the water heaters need to be replaced. We need a similar plan for our digital assets. I want to know how many items we have on different media, the average lifespan of that media, and an upgrade or replacement timeline," said Bill.

"Do you know of anyone who has created such a plan?" asked Penny.

"Off the top of my head, no," said Bill. "You could post the question in the AAM and AASLH discussion forums. People post really detailed responses. We saved a lot of time and hassle when we switched ticketing systems because those folks were so helpful."

"When do you want the plan? What do you want to do about the damaged CDs?" asked Steve.

"The budget cycle starts in a couple of months, so that's a good deadline. Let's get bids from those labs and ask them for suggestions or price quotes for transferring the rest of the collection to hard drives and the cloud. Let's get prices for printing and print storage, too," said Bill.

Steve, Penny, and Bill finished their meeting. As Steve and Penny returned to their offices, they decided who would execute which tasks. They knew their eventual plan would have to answer the following questions:

1. How does a technology maintenance plan differ from or supplement a collection management plan or a risk management plan?
2. Should the plan include cost estimates? Should cost estimates be included as a separate budget document and revised on a scheduled basis?
3. What are the advantages and disadvantages of implementing a plan for the entire Great Plains Indian Photograph Collection versus just the six damaged CD-ROMs?

Other questions to consider:

1. Which staff members should contribute to the technology maintenance plan? What role will each staff member play?
2. What criteria should be used to determine when an institution should create a technology maintenance plan?
3. What funding sources are available for museum technology projects?

CASE 3: LARSON IMMIGRATION MUSEUM

The Larson Immigration Museum has received its first grant which will fund the digitization of one thousand ship passenger logs. As IT Manager Otis Gordon and Curator Ben Ullman prepare the logs for digitization, they are surprised when volunteer Ingrid Swanson asks about the transcription of the logs. They had not considered the need for transcriptions and realize that transcriptions are needed to facilitate the use of the logs. Ingrid's suggestion of crowdsourcing the transcription is met with mixed reactions.

Museum Background

The Larson Immigration Museum was founded in 1957 to collect and share the stories of Scandinavian immigrants to Moose Lake. Founder Sven Larson was concerned that his grandchildren were losing their connection with the old country and lacked an appreciation of the hazards of the Atlantic crossing.

The Larson diligently collected oral histories and family trees. As people's interest in genealogy grew, the Larson's attendance and memberships correspondingly expanded. The budget rose to six hundred thousand dollars and had maintained that figure for eight years. Members of the local genealogy society formed the majority of the Larson's twenty-five person volunteer corps. Those volunteers conducted tours, helped visitors with research projects, and transcribed and translated documents.

The genealogy society members also donated two scanners and computer equipment to the Larson to facilitate digitization projects. Curator Ben Ullman and IT Manager Otis Gordon had prioritized the digitization projects and established a timetable for their completion. They discovered that all but one of the projects could be executed internally. The Christianson Passenger Logs consisted of one thousand ship passenger logs. Each log had twenty to one hundred pages. Other entities had digitized parts of the logs, but the Larson had the only complete collection. Otis and Ben knew that their two scanners could not process all those pages in a timely manner, so they applied for grants to have the logs professionally scanned. After four unsuccessful efforts, the fifth application was accepted. They asked volunteer Ingrid Swanson to help prepare the logs for shipment to the digitization lab.

Log Preparation

Ben, Otis, and Ingrid recorded and photographed each log as it was placed in a box, documenting the contents and conditions of the items.

"The logs are actually in pretty good shape," said Ben.

"They survived many ocean voyages, so our winters are a piece of cake," said Otis.

"The paper and bindings are so thick," said Ingrid. "I wish the books I've bought were as sturdy. The spine has already cracked on a paperback I've read once."

"Don't have to worry about that with an e-reader," said Otis.

"I had an e-reader until my husband dropped his toolbox on it," said Ingrid. "Its replacement will be my next birthday present."

"People have asked us to offer bookbinding and document repair classes," said Ben. "We're thinking about it. Our archives suppliers have kits, but have been reluctant to offer us a group rate. Jeremy is our best document repair person, but he isn't a good teacher. Katie is a good teacher and can improve her repair skills. I think we'll be able to offer something next year."

"All the genealogy society members will probably sign up. We all have papers that need some help," said Ingrid.

"What's your society project?" asked Otis.

"We're transcribing the St. Olaf church records. One priest had really horrible handwriting and wrote his records in Danish and English. It's taking forever. This project is so horrible that we are taking a six month break when it ends," said Ingrid.

"It must be bad if you all are taking a transcription break," said Ben. "You all are always indexing or transcribing something."

"Yeah, it's just too much," said Ingrid. "I feel bad because we won't be able to help you right away."

"What do you mean?" asked Otis.

"When the logs come back, we won't be able to work on the transcriptions and translations for about a year. I know how excited you are about sharing them," said Ingrid.

"You know I completely forgot about the transcription and translation," said Ben. "We were so focused on the digitization that I didn't think about that. We can start the transcriptions internally and say it's a two-year project from digitization to transcription."

"Just the transcriptions will take more than a year," said Ingrid. "Then there are the notes in multiple languages, and the occupations have to be correctly translated. If the genealogy society was in charge, we would estimate two years for the transcriptions and translations alone. Then another six months for the indexing."

"That's a long time," said Otis. "Can't you use OCR to help?"

"Nineteenth century handwriting is tough to decipher," said Ingrid. "The error rates for machine transcription and translation are pretty high. May as well do it right the first time."

"We don't want to frustrate people with inaccurate transcriptions," said Ben.

"Why don't you crowdsource the transcription?" asked Ingrid. "Genealogy sites often ask users to transcribe records. That would speed up the process."

"I read about that with the 1940 census," said Ben. "The error rates weren't bad."

"I've talked to people at national genealogy conferences. They've been pleased with the results," said Ingrid. "It definitely saved a lot of time and money. Awareness of the collections also increased."

"Sounds like a great idea," said Ben. "I'll run it by Lisa and get her thoughts. Thanks for the suggestion."

"My pleasure," said Ingrid. "Selfishly, I want easy access to the logs as fast as I can get it."

They all laughed and finished processing the shipment boxes. Ben was reasonably confident that Lisa Bergman, the museum director, would approve this proposal.

Ben and Lisa Meet

Ben and Lisa met every other Thursday to review project statuses and budget issues. This week, Ben had shipped the logs to the digitization lab and told Lisa about Ingrid's suggestion.

"I completely forgot about the transcription, because I was so focused on the digitization," said Ben.

"We all thought we would never be able to digitize those logs," said Lisa. "Transcription seemed irrelevant. We do need to make sure the digitization is well-done. The logs are in good shape now, but will need conservation over the next few years. Our storage facility needs an upgrade, too. More people are donating documents. The board and I have talked about building an addition that would be a true archive and hiring a professional archivist."

"That would be great," said Ben. "The library science and archives students have been incredibly helpful, but we only have them for a semester or two."

"Yes, we have been over-relying on the students and on the genealogy society. Both do great work, but we need the in-house expertise to properly instruct the volunteers and evaluate the work. As tempting as crowdsourcing the transcription is, I am concerned that we could lose control of the project and receive unusable results. I want to make sure people will commit to our standards, but I don't want you spending all day reviewing their work."

"I talked to some genealogy website administrators. They have been pleased with the results of their crowdsourcing projects. Some work with specific genealogy groups, rather than any site user. They do spot checks to ensure quality levels and get rid of people who are doing sloppy work.

We could ask Ingrid to suggest some other genealogy groups and provide examples of transcribed logs to set the quality standard."

"That makes sense. I think there is a state association of all the local and regional groups, too. We should talk to Ingrid first. My mother mentioned something about some of the groups not liking one another. We can't afford to alienate the majority of our volunteer pool."

"Definitely not. Even though they are self-imposing a break, I don't want them to think we are replacing them."

"Exactly. What about an ad hoc committee of museum staff and genealogy society members to manage the transcription and translation project? Then they are still involved and can work at their comfort level. We are fortunate that the society has people fluent in Danish, Finnish, Norwegian, and Swedish. I trust their translations and would feel better if they were checking the crowdsourced work."

"The language issue is my biggest concern," said Ben. "I can't double check those translations, even with Google. I'm thinking I should write something like an RFP to share with the genealogy societies and then post on our website."

"When will the logs be done?" asked Lisa.

"We will receive samples in one week. If we approve, then it will take about ten weeks. Otis needs a couple of weeks to set up the website and link it to our main site. We planned a two-week soft launch to work out the bugs and then do the big premier."

"So about twelve weeks. That should be plenty of time to work on the RFP, talk to Ingrid and the other genealogy societies, and create a plan."

"Then if we need more help, we can include that info at the premier."

Ben and Lisa agreed to that plan and timetable. As Ben began work on the RFP, he had to answer the following questions:

1. What are the roles and responsibilities of the museum staff and the genealogy society members? Should the genealogy society members have a role in actually managing the transcription and translation project?
2. What policies and procedures should be drafted to assist the potential volunteers?
3. What are the advantages and disadvantages of approaching the state genealogy association versus the individual societies?

Other questions to consider:

1. If a museum uses crowdsourcing to transcribe documents or tag photographs, should those individuals be counted as museum volunteers and held to the same standards as in-house volunteers?

2. When drafting technology project requirements, how can an institution ensure that visitor needs are incorporated?
3. What level of technology training should a curatorial staff be expected to have? What level of curatorial knowledge should the IT staff be expected to have?

EPILOGUE

Though technology presents an array of issues, both technical and behavioral, the power of technology is incredibly useful for museums and historic sites. When used effectively, technology can reduce costs and communicate with a larger audience. Like any tool, you have to read the instruction manual to learn what it can and cannot do.

The Great Plains Historical Society and the Larson Immigration Museum are using technology to preserve and share key collections. The Pike Suffrage Museum is enjoying the success of its online initiatives; the human element and the policies surrounding the use of technology are causing difficulties. As you craft your responses to the questions, consider how different generations regard various technologies and how those attitudes impact the use of technologies at museums and historic sites.

Chapter 10

Financial Planning

INTRODUCTION

The requirements of the nonprofit status and the inconstant sources of income underscore the key role of financial planning at museums and historic sites. Admissions, gift shop sales, grants, giving, endowment funds, and facility rentals are a few of the institutional revenue sources. Some sources are predictable; others are variable. Setting revenue goals, tracking income, and reviewing budget versus actuals enable museum directors and department heads to know their current financial situation and make adjustments when necessary. The public's trust in museums and historic sites extends to the financial statements. Institutions are obliged to be good stewards of their collections and their monies.

This chapter features three case studies exploring:

- the pros and cons of free admission;
- the repercussions of a failing development plan;
- people's attitudes about finances and communications; and
- the aftermath of financial improprieties.

Discussing finances can be difficult. People have different levels of risk tolerance and attitudes about spending. Those personal attitudes can have positive and negative consequences for an institution. Transparency and communication enable the discussion of those attitudes. As you develop solutions to the questions asked as the end of each case study, consider your own level of financial risk tolerance.

CASE 1: HANSEN CHILDREN'S MUSEUM

For the past three years, the Hansen Children's Museum has generated a significant profit. The "extra" money was initially used to replace old equipment and to complete wish-list projects. The positive revenue trend seems to be the new normal for the museum. Board Chair Roy Eastwood asks Museum Director Doris Hudson to revise the budget and craft a plan for the additional funds. When Doris suggests offering free admission, Roy tasks her and Financial Director John Clinton with assessing the feasibility of such a plan.

Museum Background

The Hansen Children's Museum began as an economic redevelopment project in Los Toros. The old toy factory had sat vacant for twenty years. As the town began its bicentennial plans in 1974, the mayor and councilmen were concerned that this large, vacant building overlooking the river and the town square would not be appropriately festive. Simultaneously, the town had experienced a baby boom, and parents were complaining about the lack of children's services. A children's museum was considered a constructive, educational use of the building. State and local grants were used to rehab the structure. The Hansen family, which owned the toy company, established a million dollar endowment for the museum, so the museum was named for them.

The first Hansen board wanted the museum to incorporate the different industries and cultures in Los Toros and divided the museum into sections devoted to Work, the Arts, and Peoples. Work included exhibits and activities about the toy factory, the nearby national laboratory, the farms, and the soap and beauty products factory. The Arts displayed pieces by American Indians and members of the local artist colony; local artists taught classes, too. Peoples told the stories of the American Indians, Spaniards, Danes, and Scots who lived in the area. The board also decided to keep admission fees as low as possible and to offer free admission to school groups. The primary sources of revenue were program fees, donations, memberships, facility rentals, grants, and gift shop sales; the endowment supplied the difference in any budget shortfalls.

To everyone's surprise, the Hansen was immediately financially successful. The multifaceted exhibitions and activities attracted children and adults from all of Los Toros, the nearby Indian reservation, and people from the nearby larger cities. The majority of the volunteers were schoolteachers and artists. The museum directors emphasized customer service and provided extensive training and professional development opportunities for staff and volunteers.

Museum Director Doris Hudson had been a schoolteacher and was later hired as the Hansen's education director. During her education director tenure, Doris had developed a book series about the toy factory, which was initially sold only in the Hansen's gift shop. After Doris presented the book series at the Museum Store Association conference, other museums and eventually children's bookstores asked to sell the books. The income from the book series grew to five hundred thousand dollars per year, one quarter of the annual two million dollar budget. After three years of sustained income, the board decided to regard those monies as stable and asked Doris and her team to rewrite the budget to incorporate those monies and to determine their best use. Doris and Board Chair Roy Eastwood scheduled a lunch to discuss different options.

Doris and Roy Lunch

Doris and Roy typically met every other week in the two months before the annual budget board meeting. Both were happy about their "problem" of additional income and wanted to allocate those funds in a sustainable way. Doris and Roy also believed that this income would be reliable for at least five years.

"Congratulations again on creating such popular books," said Roy.

"It was a team effort," said Doris. "Using a different local artist as the illustrator for each book has really showcased our artist colony, too. They are thrilled with the increased commissions."

"I can't believe the publisher wanted to remove the illustrations. They make the books extra special."

"They want to make the book as cheaply as possible. A friend of mine self-publishes children's books and includes photos. A publisher approached her and told her that the photos would be removed and that he would pick an illustrator for the books. She refused and is happy self-publishing and selling locally."

"That's the problem with the for-profit world—turning the special into the generic. We're proof that the special can be successful."

"You're so cynical, Roy. Still haven't been able to convince a candy company that caramel dipped beef jerky is a brilliant idea?"

"They don't know what they're missing."

"I'm sure. Sometimes ideas have to be nurtured for a while."

"I can make my own in the meantime. At least your idea has found an audience. The big question is what are we going to do with this money? We've already replaced the carpets, bought new equipment, given the staff raises, and upgraded the computers. We've actually fulfilled our ten-year wish list."

"It's a good problem to have. We have talked about giving grants."

"The board was a bit creeped out by given grants for child research. Do we want researchers following the kids around the museum, writing down everything they do?"

"The research doesn't have to be done on-site, and we can set the parameters for the types of projects to be funded. My concerns are that we would need to build a new department specifically for that purpose and that our community wouldn't directly benefit. Free admission is a popular topic right now. I think we could offer that benefit."

"How much does admission contribute now?"

"About a quarter of the budget, so it would be an even swap."

"Do people value something they get for free?"

"That is one of the questions. Some museums are using a 'pay-as-you-will' model, which reminds people that museums do have expenses. It also allows people to contribute according to their means."

"I like 'pay-as-you-will.' People can have crazy expectations for free stuff. Our society is forgetting that nothing is free. There is always a cost. Can you have John run some numbers for us? Run one scenario with the even swap and then other scenarios with different levels of contribution based on the current admissions revenue."

"Yes, he and I are meeting this afternoon. I had also asked him to create projections for the book series revenues—at some point, that income will decline. He was doing some research about that drop off."

"Great," said Roy. "John is pretty pessimistic, so we'll definitely get the worst case scenarios."

Roy and Doris finished their lunch, optimistic about the possibility of offering free admission to the Hansen.

Doris and John Meet

Doris explained to John her thoughts about free admission and pay-as-you-will. She also relayed Roy's request for scenarios.

"This is very risky," said John. "Our admission contribution is relatively stable. The book income should start to decline in two years. You'll have to develop a new series to keep that income at that level. Are you giving free admission to everyone? Why not just city or state residents? Then we are benefiting the real community members."

"That's a good point," said Doris. "We can discuss selective free admission with the board. As I recall, 70 percent of our visitors are local, so we may as well offer free admission to everyone."

"I will double check those numbers. What about membership benefits? Free admission is one of the key selling points."

"That is another wrinkle. We can offer free passes to two or three programs, depending on the level of membership."

"I'll have to account for that revenue loss, too. We could lose a lot of money offering free admission."

"Our current problem is the consistently large amount of income from the book series. We've upgraded, enhanced, and revamped everything that we can."

"That's true," said John. "We can't keep accruing large amounts of money without an allocation."

"We have avoided using the endowment for the past few years," said Doris. "So we are building our nest egg and will be able to supplement any short-term income differences."

"That's true. The endowment has been growing nicely."

"We want to avoid the problems that the arts foundation had."

"That's true. We don't want to be accused of hoarding money or enjoying champagne lunches at five-star restaurants. I'll run different scenarios using all the variables we discussed. Maybe free admission won't be too bad."

"Let's be optimistic," said Doris.

As John began working on the scenarios, Doris realized that he had raised key issues about the effects of free admission or pay-as-you-will on other aspects of the museum financials. She knew that she needed answers to the following questions before the board meeting:

1. Is swapping the book income for the admission income an even swap? Why or why not?
2. What other benefits could the membership program offer?
3. How else could the extra book income be allocated?

Other questions to consider:

1. What other income sources are affected by the introduction of a free admission or pay-as-you-will initiative?
2. Which criteria or metrics should be used in deciding to implement a free admission or pay-as-you-will initiative?
3. What is the relationship between paying admission and valuing/appreciating a museum?

CASE 2: THORNE ART MUSEUM

The Thorne Art Museum is in the third year of a five-year building project. The actual donations for the project are much less than the projected donations. A new auditor questions the project expenses and refuses to approve the financial statement. Museum Director Daniel Yerkes is caught in the middle of a battle between Board Chair Samuel Burnham, who wants to proceed at any cost, and the Head of the Board Finance Committee Ernst Marshall, who wants to reduce the construction costs.

Museum Background

The Thorne Art Museum has been the key cultural institution in Springfield, since its inception in 1873. The city's elite controlled the thirty-person board and enjoyed champagne and caviar lunches. They did not enjoy giving requirements and refused to implement them. Board members believed that a one-time bequest and occasional art donations were sufficient. Board seats remained within the original families with an occasional offer to a nouveau riche person deemed acceptable through significant donations. The museum staff understood that the familial quirks of the board members must be accommodated—a trade-off for the higher than typical museum salaries and institutional financial stability.

Funds for the seventy million dollar annual operating budget were derived from admissions, memberships, non-board giving, gift shop sales, grants, facility rentals, the endowment, and licensing fees. The endowment funds were managed conservatively. People with for-profit experience were hired to manage the gift shop, licensing, and facility rental departments.

The New Wing

As the twenty-year anniversary of Board Chair Samuel Burnham's tenure approached, the board decided to build a new wing, named for Burnham. The wing would house classical sculpture, which was Burnham's favorite type of art. The project was budgeted at one hundred thirty-five million dollars to ensure that the design and finishes blended with the marble, onyx, and limestone used in the original building.

Museum Director Daniel Yerkes was concerned about the new wing. None of the board members had committed to specific donations for the wing. The director of development told Daniel that some board members thought the wing should be dedicated to contemporary art and therefore refused to donate money for the construction. A few board members did not like Burnham personally, so they refused to donate money. Burnham's friends donated ten million dollars. By the time construction began, donations totaled twenty-seven million dollars, far less than the 50 percent recommended for beginning such a project. Now three years in to the five-year project, the donations stalled at sixty million dollars.

Another issue was the new auditor. In years past, the museum's finances were audited by Ken Anderson, a friend of Samuel Burnham. Ken was unconcerned about the fundraising shortfall and approved the museum's finances.

He had retired, and Arthur Young, the new auditor, had no personal ties to any board members. Daniel was pleased about Arthur's independence, but concerned about the potential repercussions of that neutrality as he entered the room for their first meeting.

"The main museum statements are well done. We are in compliance with the tax codes, and the documentation is excellent. I was able to review the materials quickly and to understand all of the calculations and statements," said Arthur. "It was a pleasure to see such good recordkeeping."

"Thank you," said Daniel. "We emphasize fiscal management and compliance skills with our staff. Art museums are cost-intensive, so we try to be as efficient as possible. I would imagine other nonprofits have a similar point of view."

"You would be surprised. The issues are usually lack of accounting knowledge and inexperience with endowment investing. If you don't know what a derivative swap is, don't use it for your endowment. If you are a non-profit, you shouldn't use risky and complicated investment tools regardless. I was impressed that your endowment survived the economic downturn reasonably well."

"We used to be criticized for our conservative investment philosophy. Now we are praised. After a few more years of economic stability, I'm sure we'll be criticized again."

"Ignore that critique. The main museum finances are in good shape. If I only had to approve those finances, I would sign off on them. However, I am having difficulties with the new wing and its impact on the main museum finances. So I will not be able to approve the financial statements."

"For the record, can you tell me what those issues are?"

"Yes, the executive summary of my report bullet points the items, too. The major issue is the seventy-five million dollar donation shortfall for the new wing. The bulk of the money was donated in the first two years. Last year saw ten million dollars in donations. Receiving the remainder of those funds via giving within the next two years is improbable. The terms of the endowment allow you to tap 10 percent of the principal for a capital construction project every twenty years, which would contribute thirty million dollars."

"So we would be at ninety million dollars," said Daniel.

"Correct. I reviewed the budget for the wing and spoke with some experts. If you substitute polished concrete for the remaining marble and onyx finishes, a café for the full service restaurant, and educational areas for gallery space, you should be able to remain within a ninety million dollar budget and reduce your subsequent additional operating expenses by 30 percent," said Arthur.

"Honestly, I would rather have educational areas than the gallery space. We have plenty of gallery space. I don't think the board will be enthusiastic about the suggestions."

"The current financials are not feasible. I will not sign off on the financial statement until the seventy-five million dollar shortfall is addressed. You do not have the money to pay the construction team at the end of this month."

"I appreciate your candor," said Daniel.

Daniel and Arthur wrapped up their meeting. Daniel had hoped that Ken would have raised these issues last year with Samuel and persuaded his friend to adjust the budget. Samuel did not react well to people telling him what to do, especially people he didn't know. Since the Burnham name would be on the wing, Daniel suspected that compromise would be difficult.

The Financial Committee Meeting

After the auditor reviewed the results with the museum director, the next step was for the museum director, board chair, and the head of the Board Finance Committee to meet and review the auditor's statement before it would be presented at the subsequent board meeting. Samuel had already notified Daniel and Ernst Marshall, the head of the Board Finance Committee, that he would be late. Daniel appreciated the opportunity to speak with Ernst, who was an independent voice on the board.

"The auditor's report doesn't surprise me," said Ernst. "We should have adjusted the budget when funding stalled last year or opened up the wing to other art. Who wants to see four floors of marble sculptures?"

"We have a large collection," said Daniel. "Sculpture is difficult to move. We had some unfortunate breakage deinstalling our Cupid and Psyche exhibition. The floor reinforcement has already been installed, so we can put any heavy artifact in the wing."

"I'm partial to a World War II tank exhibit."

"The floor could withstand it. The doors would be too small. What do you think of Arthur's construction suggestions?"

"I'm fine with the concrete, but I think we can make money with the restaurant. The cost of our board parties will be cheaper with an in-house restaurant."

"We do have a lot of board events, so achieving a savings would be helpful. How do you think Samuel will react to Arthur's refusal to approve the audit?"

"He'll fire him and get someone who will rubber stamp it. Arthur's report is part of the official financials, regardless, so the board has to address it in some way."

"I suspect the rest of the board will agree with Samuel."

"He's the chair, and most people really don't care about the museum. They just like the prestige of being on the board. Sorry."

"Yes, I fully recognize that reality."

"What reality?" asked Samuel, as he entered the meeting room.

"We all have different passions and interests," said Daniel.

"That is very true," said Samuel. "Is the auditor's report ready?"

"Well, there are a few problems," said Ernst, who proceeded to summarize Arthur's concerns, as Samuel flipped through the report.

"He clearly doesn't understand non-profit financials," said Samuel. "Ken was comfortable with the wing's financials. There's always a lull around the midpoint. When people can start to see what the finished wing will look like, they'll be inspired to give."

"That's true, up to a point," said Ernst. "You know half of the board isn't going to give a dime to this thing. They usually fill the fundraising gap as a project is completed."

"They will want their names on the bronze plaque once they actually see the wing. I looked in on it this morning. The onyx and alabaster are stunning," said Samuel. "They might have preferred to put modern art there, but they will want their names on it when the architecture critics review the space. Besides we can pull money from the endowment. Arthur admits that."

"The construction exemption caps the contribution at thirty million dollars. I checked the bylaws. The appropriation still must be approved by two-thirds of the board," said Daniel.

Ernst laughed, and Samuel glared. Both knew that achieving a two-thirds majority would be incredibly difficult. Touching the principal of the endowment would set a precedent that some board members would loathe—even if the bylaws allowed such a transaction.

"So I think you need to revamp your development staff, Daniel," said Samuel. "Clearly, they could not manage such a large project."

"With all due respect, the development staff has done an excellent job," said Daniel. "Over the past ten years, they have raised five hundred million dollars for various campaigns and shepherded the endowment through a difficult economic environment. Other museums have tried to recruit them."

"How much have you donated, Samuel?" asked Ernst.

"I can't donate. The wing is a tribute to me. Donating would be self-aggrandizing," said Samuel.

"What about all your banker friends? Surely, they have contributed," said Ernst.

"My friendship isn't for sale," said Samuel. "People actually like me."

"Returning to the report," said Daniel, "we need a response to Arthur's comments. Accessing the endowment should be proposed, with an accompanying list of pros and cons. We can also re-examine the wing budget and identify substitutions for higher cost items."

"Concrete is déclassé," said Samuel.

"Please, you didn't even recognize that Wright used concrete on that tour. You thought it was a natural stone," said Ernst.

"Frank Lloyd Wright is merely a modern architect," said Samuel, "I expect such shenanigans from him. We have a classical building and must use classical materials."

"I'll obtain samples in case anyone on the board asks to see the difference," said Daniel.

"How would they even know about it," said Samuel.

"The auditor himself sends copies of his report to all of the board members," said Daniel. "That policy was instituted after the unfortunate incident in 1978."

"Wasn't your father involved in that, Samuel?" said Ernst.

"So everyone will have received their copy by now and may require some clarifications or additional information," said Daniel. "I think copies of the wing budget should also be available for review."

"You need to figure out how to finish this wing," said Samuel. "We're three years in. If you can't handle the job, I'll find someone who can."

"Stop threatening people's jobs," said Ernst. "Daniel is working on options for your temple. The reality is that you may have to compromise. You're never going to get the two-thirds vote for the thirty million. The board is theoretically responsible for fundraising, too. You're the Chair, so make some calls."

"You are pushing too hard," said Samuel.

"Don't threaten the livelihoods of the museum staff," said Ernst.

"Well, I think we have accomplished all we can at this meeting," said Daniel. "I'll work on the materials for the main board meeting next week. If either of you have any other suggestions or thoughts, please let me know."

Daniel breathed a sigh of relief as Samuel and Ernst left the room without further discussion. Today's meeting had been a preview of the passions Daniel expected at the next board meeting. As he returned to his office, Daniel knew that Arthur was correct. The costs for the wing would have to be reduced, and the thirty million dollars from the endowment was not assured. Daniel knew their eventual plan would have to answer the following questions:

1. Why should the board vote for the use of the endowment?
2. Which major line items should be eliminated or adjusted: the restaurant, the marble finishes, the large gallery spaces? How?
3. Would repurposing the wing from a sculpture gallery to a nonspecific collection gallery aid the fundraising campaign? Why or why not?

Other questions to consider:

1. In what circumstances could a capital project began if the funds raised are less than the 50 percent recommended benchmark?
2. Given the fundraising issues, could the development staff have used any other tactics or strategies?
3. Who should be held responsible if the wing is a financial disaster?

CASE 3: TROUT AUTOMOBILE MUSEUM

After an audit, the board at the Trout Automobile Museum discovered that Museum Director Dick Anthony had improperly used museum funds. Anthony resigned, and Assistant Director Grace Wilbur has been promoted to museum director. Grace and the board must now establish new financial protocols and decide how to present the situation to the museum members and the general public. They also have to decide about formally pressing charges against Dick Anthony. Grace and the museum staff believe full disclosure is essential to maintaining the public trust. Board Chair Tony Mott is concerned about damage to the museum's reputation.

Museum Background

The Trout Automobile Museum was the private automobile collection of Seth Trout, a local automobile dealer who began collecting cars in the 1960s. When Trout retired from the automobile business in 1980, he decided to turn his dealership into a showcase for his collection. That showcase eventually turned into the Trout Automobile Museum.

Seth Trout's collection was well-respected, consisting of US and foreign cars—rare and representative examples. The Trout mechanic staff was often consulted about repairs and restorations. People from around the world visited the museum, located in the small town of Rockport. Attendance averaged five hundred thousand per year. Most of the three million dollar budget was spent on the maintenance of the vehicles. The Trout also maintained a small track to drive the cars in a protected environment. The annual Running of the Cars was the museum's most popular program and Rockport's biggest tourist attraction.

The Trout was a major employer in the town and a key part of its economy. The hotels and restaurants depended on the Trout's visitors. Students and working mothers relied on part-time work at the Trout to fund their education and to supplement their family income, respectively. The board understood the importance of the Trout to the community and carefully considered the impact of their actions on their fellow citizens.

The Discovery

Every five years, the board hired an accounting firm to conduct a thorough audit of the books. The regular accountant performed basic checks annually. The more thorough audit was a precautionary measure. The Trout's collection and parts inventory were valued in the millions, so its insurance company appreciated that extra level of review. There had never been an issue with the Trout passing the audit.

Museum Director Dick Anthony had been at the Trout for eight years and had therefore experienced an audit. Anthony also had a small collection of antique cars and frequently asked the mechanics for advice about his cars. He sometimes tried to persuade the mechanics to stop by his house and look at his cars. They refused, and he would stop asking for a few months. Approximately a year ago, Dick asked Hank Tucker, the head mechanic, to give him the supply orders for submission to the vendors. Dick told Hank that the board wanted this additional layer of checking to make sure the mechanics weren't ordering parts for themselves. Hank was offended that anyone would think his staff would commit such acts, but acquiesced to Dick's request. Hank did not know that Dick had lied and wanted to add his own supply needs to the museum requests. When the shipments arrived, Dick would remove his parts from the warehouse at night before the items were entered into the museum's inventory system.

During the audit, the auditors compared the original supply orders to the inventory. After noting anomalies from the previous audit's supply orders, the auditors asked the mechanics about the new parts. The mechanics told the auditors that the parts were not used on any of the cars in the collection. After a mechanic offhandedly mentioned that one of Dick's cars had needed one of the parts, the auditors began investigating him.

After presenting their evidence to the board and Dick, the auditors recommended criminal charges. Dick offered to pay back the museum and resign. The board accepted his resignation and repayment, but remained unsure about the criminal charges. They promoted Grace Wilbur, the assistant director, to museum director. Board Chair Tony Mott scheduled a meeting with Grace to explain the entire situation.

Tony and Grace Meet

"Now you have the full story," said Tony. "I'll understand if you want to refuse the promotion."

"Of course not," said Grace. "I've worked at the Trout since I graduated from college. We can't let one unfortunate occurrence deter us. The question is how to move forward. The rumor mill is already buzzing. Dick has left town."

"He'll be back," said Tony. "He went to Bellford to find a good lawyer and to sell a couple of his cars to pay for the lawyer. He wasn't too happy."

"He shouldn't have stolen the parts," said Grace. "It's his own fault."

"We all make mistakes," said Tony.

"Mistakes and crimes are different," said Grace. "He violated the public trust and our trust. His actions have repercussions."

"The board really doesn't want a scandal. People respect the museum, and we failed them."

"Nonsense. We justified their trust. The auditing process uncovered the problem, as it was meant to do. The board affected swift action. The next steps are criminal charges and sharing the story."

"Criminal charges would be scandalous. Sharing the story makes us look bad."

"If we let him get away with fraud at our museum, we are allowing him the opportunity to do the same thing at another museum," said Grace. "He will probably steal more the next time because he got away with it here. We have a moral and ethical obligation to protect other institutions. Allowing someone to get away with a crime is scandalous."

"He might sue us for slander."

"He can't sue us for turning over evidence to the prosecutor, who then decides if there is enough evidence to press changes. Truth is an absolute defense. If he wants to sue us, he will have to submit to discovery and an affidavit. I don't think he will do that."

"We just need to stop the rumors."

"We can stop the rumors by explaining the situation. Let's turn the evidence over to the prosecutors and make a public statement."

After a further discussion, Grace and Tony decided to speak with the Trout's marketing director, Gloria Curtis, and the finance director, Susan Chapman.

The Staff Meeting

Grace and Tony explained the situation to Gloria and Susan. Tony presented the board's point of view, and Grace gave her thoughts. All agreed that the townspeople would have strong reactions to the situation.

"The rumor mill is already in overdrive," said Gloria. "From a public relations perspective, telling the truth allows us to present the reality of the situation. He defrauded us of twenty thousand dollars in parts. By tomorrow morning, someone could say he stole two hundred thousand dollars from the endowment. Then the community would really lose faith in us."

"Twenty thousand dollars is a considerable sum," said Susan. "That's a felony. I agree with Grace. He needs to experience the consequences of his actions."

"The negative community reaction could affect fundraising and attendance," said Tony. "People won't trust us with their money."

"In the short term, possibly. They definitely won't trust us if we don't report the crime," said Grace.

"We're not the only museum to have this experience," said Gloria. "I read about a museum director who spent over a half a million dollars on museum credit cards on personal items. From what I have read in my marketing publications, the institutions who publicly present the situation and press charges are the institutions who maintain community respect. The institutions who try to hide the situation are the ones who lose the community's trust, especially if the person commits the same crime at another museum."

"Yes," said Susan. "My finance journals are also publishing more case studies and stories about internal theft to help us catch the problems as soon as possible. It's embarrassing when it happens to you, but our protocols did catch the problem."

"What else could we do to prevent it from happening again?" asked Tony.

"Dick's ruse was actually a good idea. Someone else should check the supply orders for fraud," said Grace. "Both Hank and I could sign the orders in one another's presence."

"Let's review our protocols," said Gloria. "Then when we issue our public statement, we can say how we are trying to prevent a recurrence of the same situation."

"The board would appreciate that," said Tony.

"Gloria, Susan, and I can work on a public statement and protocols, based on such incidents at other museums," said Grace. "Then we can present that material to the board and the museum lawyer tomorrow afternoon. Afterward, we can meet with the prosecutor and make a public statement."

"That seems a little fast," said Tony.

"The longer we wait, the crazier the rumor mill," said Grace. "Let's just get it over with and move forward."

Though Tony wasn't happy with the timeline, he agreed to contact the rest of the board and the Trout's lawyer for a meeting the following afternoon. Grace, Gloria, and Susan began working on a protocol proposal and a public statement, which would answer the following questions:

1. Why is the museum presenting the evidence to the public prosecutor?
2. How can the museum prevent a similar situation in the future?
3. What should the museum say in its public statement?

Other questions to consider:

1. How can the museum balance its moral, ethical, and legal obligation to report a crime with its concerns about admitting a betrayal of the public trust?
2. What are the consequences of making a public statement about financial crimes?
3. Should associations for museums or nonprofits provide training or guidelines for managing the public consequences of museum staff criminal behavior?

EPILOGUE

Income is the fuel that enables museums and historic sites to affect their missions. The public expects responsible and transparent money management. As with for-profit institutions, mistakes, unwillingness to believe data, and fraud occur. Concerns about institutional reputation and personal feelings can obfuscate moral, ethical, and legal obligations.

The Hansen Children's Museum is experiencing a surprise financial success and is trying to share that success with its community. The Thorne Art Museum and the Trout Automobile Museum are enduring financial problems. The attitudes of the people involved are affecting the possible solutions; the actual financials may appear to be an afterthought, rather than the key concern. As you craft your responses to the questions, consider the gap between the realities of the financial statements and people's perceptions of those realities.

Summation

The art museums, historical societies, science museums, historic homes, botanic gardens, planetariums, history museums, and children's museums represented in these fictionalized real-life case studies all grapple with:

- establishing policies, procedures, and expectations;
- changing people's attitudes;
- interacting with their communities;
- defining success versus failure;
- dealing with the repercussions of past decisions; and
- allocating financial and personnel resources.

The interpersonal dynamics among the staff, volunteers, board members, and other community members determined the level of cooperation or animosity, which then impacted both the discussions and resolutions of the problems.

Miscommunication and misunderstanding intermingle throughout the cases. Miscommunication takes the form of vague or nonexistent policies, information omission, and assumptions. Misunderstanding can be seen in the gap between technically correct best practices and ethics versus a non-practitioner perspective, the different experience levels of personnel, and a disconnect between mission and public expectation. Miscommunication and misunderstanding can be deliberate or unintentional. If the actions are deliberate, then the decisions will fail. If unintentional situations can be improved, and decisions can be successful. Honest, direct communication identifies multiple options for resolving problems and assesses the risk in each option.

Within an institution, people trained in the methodologies and standards appropriate to their professions coexist. In chapter 2, case 3, the Cameron History Museum, the protagonists grapple with the implications of the

Association of Fundraising Professionals Code of Ethics on the potential tasks assigned to a professional fundraising consultant. Respect for the other person's professionalism and professional standard is essential. Professionals may disagree; mutual respect is enforced through adherence to standards, which establish the base level of practices and methods, regardless of project or issue. Each of those methodologies and standards are valid and valuable. These different standards and best practices provide needed parameters and options in decision-making.

After reading the cases and discussing them in a group setting, the individual interpretations of the problems to be solved and the possible resolutions may vary greatly. The nature of the case study approach is to unearth the complexity in seemingly discrete decisions. The goal of these case studies is to underscore the necessity of persuasion to implement the solution. Though the specific details of these case studies may become irrelevant over time, the basic conflicts among the protagonists that are rooted in personality clashes, misunderstandings, and miscommunications will remain.

Learning how to communicate with different personality types is a long-standing challenge. Daniel Yerkes, the museum director in chapter 10, case 2, Thorne Art Museum, is sandwiched between two vociferous board members who are equally convinced that the other has failed his fiduciary duty. Daniel remains focused on the problem at hand and does not participate in the arguments and accusations. He returns the discussion to the issue at hand, but does allow people to express their frustrations. Daniel has obviously had years of experience in managing passionate arguments. Gail Burr, the young and inexperienced museum director in chapter 1, case 2, Burmilana County Historical Society, is having difficulties communicating instructions to her nonprofessional volunteer staff. Even though the board assigned a mentor to assist Gail in the transition from worker to manager, Gail's desire to implement professional standards and practices overrode her need to improve her communication skills. Gail failed to recognize that the volunteers wanted to follow her instructions, but couldn't due to her inarticulateness. The inability to work with or understand different personality types or communication styles will limit your career.

Some people are naturally perceptive or persuasive. Others may always have difficulties with public speaking or interpreting others. Everyone can use the analytical tools discussed in the introduction to create effective arguments. The Blindspot Analysis, SWOT Analysis, and Risk Mitigation Plan facilitate the analysis of the problem at hand and its potential solutions and offer a physical template that can be used in reports or presentations. Their structure helps you organize your thoughts in a logical and rational manner. The management literature bursts with other useful tools, templates, and analytical techniques, which can be adapted for use by nonprofit institutions.

These tools are dynamic and useful when applied correctly. You can experiment with different tools and techniques to fully understand their applicability. Your personal professional development plan can explore these different tools and techniques to successfully manage responsibilities and to improve communication skills.

PROFESSIONAL DEVELOPMENT

Each person has opportunities to identify strengths and weaknesses and to create a self-education plan. Additional degrees or certifications can provide a deeper base of professional knowledge. Conferences, associations, and social media groups create a network of fellow professionals who can suggest solutions or empathize with difficulties. Organizations like Toastmasters or local adult education classes offer opportunities to improve communication skills. Reading professional journals in museology, nonprofit management, and subject-specific disciplines also expand your base of knowledge and challenge you to develop a point of view about current trends and key issues.

Institutions are both the sum of their staff and an entity in and of themselves. Meetings, retreats, and daily interactions create the institutional culture. The size or type of institution does not necessarily dictate that culture. A small staff led by a controlling director may endure a more restrictive environment than a large staff led by a collaborative leader. Realistically, an institution can only change if the leadership incentivizes change. Each individual still has the choice to act according to professional standards and ethics.

THE MUSEUM-PUBLIC HISTORY PROFESSION

The Museum-Public History profession itself also evolves via internal self-reflection and external forces. In chapter 9, case 1, Pike Suffrage Museum, the protagonists discuss the impact of the Internet on their audience and mission. That case explicitly asks: Should museums adjust their mission statements to clarify their in-person and online missions? Additional questions are: How can a museum accommodate its in-person and online audiences? Should the in-person audience be explicitly prioritized over the online audience?

Realistically, every institution has limited resources and must prioritize. The needs of the general public versus scholars are different, providing a parallel for the in-person versus online audience. The priority could be for people who actively engage with the institution's mission or collection and then demonstrate that engagement, as defined by the institution.

Social media provides a multimedia platform for the audience and the institution. A teacher could use educational materials from a museum on the other side of the world and post a video of the resulting class projects, which could inspire another teacher to use those materials or another person to visit the museum. A digitized collection could enable a scholarly breakthrough. If the institution is unaware of those specific impacts, determining project priorities is difficult. Feedback from in-person guests and social media tracking statistics are the available metrics upon which to base decisions.

Visitor expectations have altered, as well. "Checking in" on Facebook to notify friends that you are at a museum is a common activity. Posting photos of oneself with artifacts on Instagram or live tweeting reactions to an exhibition are activities that are sometimes encouraged by museums or historic sites. While individual institutions may have greater difficulties setting boundaries for such activities due to the nature of their collections, the issues can no longer be avoided. Public history uses the concept of shared authority, whereby both the history/museum professional and the layperson contribute to the historical narrative. Social media enables such contributions or collaborations, which visitors now expect and which institutions can channel. In essence, the volunteer pool is now global. Documents can be transcribed or translated; people in pictures can be recognized; tools or objects can be identified. Crowdsourcing can help institutions mitigate the impact from reduced financial resources or fast-track stalled projects. Though technology and visitor expectations are ever-changing, museum and public history professionals remain responsible for integrating those changes into their institutions.

THE FUTURE OF MUSEUMS AND HISTORIC SITES

Museums and historic sites are places of education, inspiration, exploration, and connection. They are community meeting spaces that help people understand social, cultural, and civic issues. They facilitate the public discourse and preserve the collective past with relatively small staff and budgets, disproportionate to their missions. Decision-making and communication skills are, therefore, critical.

I hope the immersive nature of these thirty case studies have provoked strong reactions and helped you better understand yourself or your colleagues. Use these cases to think about how you would emotionally react in a similar situation and then work toward a solution. Challenges and uncertainties occur daily. How we handle those challenges and uncertainties determines our success or failure. Individual and collective success is achieved when a group of people respect one another, work toward a common mission, and agree on general protocols and procedures.

Appendix
Case Studies by Institution Type

ART MUSEUM

- Chapter 1, Case 3: Wilis Art Museum
- Chapter 2, Case 2: Putnam Art Museum
- Chapter 4, Case 1: Byrd Art Museum
- Chapter 7, Case 2: Corbett Art Museum
- Chapter 10, Case 2: Thorne Art Museum

BOTANIC GARDEN/NATURE MUSEUM

- Chapter 3, Case 2: The Copperfield Botanical Garden
- Chapter 4, Case 2: Lloyd Natural History Museum
- Chapter 5, Case 1: Lampe Nature Museum

CHILDREN'S MUSEUM

- Chapter 1, Case 1: Gerdes Children's Museum
- Chapter 6, Case 1: Barton Children's Museum
- Chapter 10, Case 1: Hansen Children's Museum

HISTORIC HOUSE MUSEUM

- Chapter 3, Case 1: James Benjamin House Museum

HISTORICAL SOCIETY

- Chapter 1, Case 2: Burmilana County Historical Society
- Chapter 3, Case 3: Berlin Historical Society
- Chapter 4, Case 3: Chandlerville Historical Society
- Chapter 5, Case 3: Quentin Historical Society
- Chapter 9, Case 2: Great Plains Historical Society

HISTORY MUSEUM

- Chapter 2, Case 3: Cameron History Museum
- Chapter 5, Case 2: Perske History Museum
- Chapter 9, Case 1: Pike Suffrage Museum
- Chapter 9, Case 3: Larson Immigration Museum

PLANETARIUM

- Chapter 6, Case 3: Stone-Parker Planetarium

SCIENCE MUSEUM

- Chapter 2, Case 1: Lewton Science Museum
- Chapter 6, Case 2: Norman Science Museum

SPECIALTY MUSEUM

- Chapter 7, Case 1: Owens Veteran's Museum
- Chapter 7, Case 3: Caron Cartographic Society
- Chapter 8, Case 1: Abraham Music Box Museum
- Chapter 8, Case 2: Moore Theatre Museum
- Chapter 8, Case 3: Harrison Miniature House Museum
- Chapter 10, Case 3: Trout Automobile Museum

Resource List

MANAGEMENT BOOKS

Beckwith, Harry. *Selling the Invisible: A Field Guide to Modern Marketing.* New York: Warner Books, 1997.

Bossidy, Larry, and Ram Charan. *Execution: The Discipline of Getting Things Done.* New York: Crown Business, 2002.

US Marine Corps. *Warfighting: The U.S. Marine Corps Book of Strategy.* New York: Doubleday, 1994.

MUSEUM MANAGEMENT PUBLICATIONS

American Association for Museum Volunteers. "Standards and Best Practices for Museum Volunteer Programs." http://www.aamv.org/resources/standards-and-best-practices/.

Catlin-Legutko, Cinnamon, and Stacy Klingler, eds. *Small Museum Toolkit.* Lanham, MD: AltaMira Press, 2012.

Center for the Future of Museums. "Trendswatch." http://www.aam-us.org/resources/center-for-the-future-of-museums/projects-and-reports/trendswatch.

Cilela Jr., Salvatore G. *Fundraising for Small Museums: In Good Times and Bad.* Lanham, MD: AltaMira Press, 2011.

Johnson, Anna, Kimberly A. Huber, Nancy Cutler, Melissa Bingmann, and Tim Grove. *The Museum Educator's Manual: Educators Share Successful Techniques.* Lanham, MD: AltaMira Press, 2009.

Lord, Barry, Gail Dexter Lord, and Lindsay Martin, eds. *Manual of Museum Planning: Sustainable Space, Facilities, and Operations.* 3rd ed. Lanham, MD: AltaMira Press, 2012.

Malaro, Maria C., and Ildiko Pogany DeAngelis. *A Legal Primer on Managing Museum Collections.* 3rd ed. Washington, DC: Smithsonian Books, 2012.

National Association of Interpretation. "Standards and Practices for Interpretive Methods." Fort Collins: National Association of Interpretation, 2009.

Schmickle, Bill. *The Politics of Historic Districts: A Primer for Grassroots Preservation.* Lanham, MD: AltaMira Press, 2007.

Serrell, Beverly. *Exhibit Labels: An Interpretive Approach.* Lanham, MD: AltaMira Press, 1996.

Simon, Nina. *Museum 2.0 Blog.* http://museumtwo.blogspot.com.

PROFESSIONAL ASSOCIATIONS—MUSEUM

American Alliance of Museums. http://www.aam-us.org.

American Association for Museum Volunteers. http://www.aamv.org.

American Association for State and Local History. http://www.aaslh.org.

American Public Gardens Association. http://www.publicgardens.org.

Association for Living History, Farm and Agricultural Museums. http://www.alhfam.org.

Association of Art Museum Directors. https://http://www.aamd.org.

Association of Children's Museums. http://www.childrensmuseums.org.

Association of Fundraising Professionals." http://www.afpnet.org.

Association of Nature Center Administrators. http://www.natctr.org.

Association of Science and Technology Centers. http://www.astc.org.

Emerging Museum Professionals: Facebook Group. http://www.facebook.com/groups/5777503793/.

Institute of Museum and Library Services. http://www.imls.gov.

International Planetarium Society. http://www.ips-planetarium.org.

Museum-Ed: Connecting the Museum Educator Community. http://museum-ed.org.

National Council on Public History. http://www.ncph.org.

PROFESSIONAL ASSOCIATIONS—OTHER

American Bar Association. http://www.americanbar.org/.

American Institute of Certified Public Accountants. http://www.aicpa.org.

Boardsource: Exceptional Governance Practices for Nonprofit Boards." https://http://www.boardsource.org/.

Center for Nonprofit Management. http://www.cnm.org.

Foundation Center: Tools and Resources for Philanthropy and the Social Sector. http://foundationcenter.org.

SOFTWARE AND WEB RESOURCES

Dplan: The Online Disaster Planning Tool for Cultural and Civic Institutions. Northeast Document Conservation Center. http://www.dplan.org.

Indiegogo: The Largest Global Crowdfunding & Fundraising Site Online. http://
www.indiegogo.com.
Omeka Web Publishing Software. https://omeka.org.
Pastperfect Museum Software. http://www.museumsoftware.com.
Pew Research Center: Polling and Demographic Research. http://www.pewresearch.org.
Preservation Directory. http://www.preservationdirectory.com.
Prezi Presentation Software. https://prezi.com.
Toastmasters International. https://http://www.toastmasters.org.
TripAdvisor. http://www.tripadvisor.com.

Index

161

About the Author

Samantha Chmelik is a public historian at Preston Argus, LLC. She has worked and volunteered at libraries, museums, and nonprofit organizations for two decades, developing areas of expertise in research, project management, strategic planning, and best practices/benchmarking. Her historical research has been published by the German Historical Institute and presented at the Organization of American Historians/National Council on Public History Conference and the Business History Conference; her articles about benchmarking and strategic planning have been published in *Information Outlook* and *Intelligence Insights*. After receiving a BA from Wellesley College, Chmelik then earned an MS in library and information science from Simmons GSLIS, an MBA from the University of Illinois at Chicago, and an MA in public history from Loyola University, Chicago.